HIDDEN STIRLING

Murray Cook

Other Books by Murray Cook

Rituals, Roundhouses and Romans
[with Lindsay Dunbar]

Digging into Stirling's Past:
Uncovering the Secrets of Scotland's Smallest City

The Anvil of Scottish History: Stories of Stirling

Balbithan Wood, Kintore, Aberdeenshire:
The Evaluation of Prehistoric Landscapes

White Castle:
The Evaluation of an Upstanding Prehistoric Enclosure in East Lothian
[with David Connolly and Hana Kdolska]

Bannockburn and Stirling Bridge:
Exploring Scotland's Two Greatest Battles

The Bannock Burn:
Journeys Along and Across the World's Most Famous Burn
[with Ian McNeish]

Scotland's Christmas:
Festive Celebrations, Traditions and Customs in Scotland
from Samhain to Still Game
[with Thomas A. Christie]

Conflicts of the Forth:
Exploring 6,000 Years of Warfare at Scotland's Bloodiest Spot
[with Jim Roche]

HIDDEN STIRLING

Outlawed, Unknown, Locked, Destroyed, Overlooked and Secret Gems from Scotland's Smallest City

Murray Cook

Extremis publishing

Hidden Stirling: Outlawed, Unknown, Locked, Destroyed, Overlooked and Secret Gems from Scotland's Smallest City by Murray Cook.

First edition published in Great Britain in 2025 by Extremis Publishing Ltd., Suite 218, Castle House, 1 Baker Street, Stirling, FK8 1AL, United Kingdom.

www.extremispublishing.com

Extremis Publishing is a Private Limited Company registered in Scotland (SC509983) whose Registered Office is Suite 218, Castle House, 1 Baker Street, Stirling, FK8 1AL, United Kingdom.

Copyright © Murray Cook, 2025.

Murray Cook has asserted the moral right under the Copyright, Designs and Patents Act 1988 to be identified as the authors of this work.

The views expressed in this work are solely those of the author, and do not necessarily reflect those of the publisher. The publisher hereby disclaims any responsibility for them.

This book is a work of non-fiction. Unless otherwise noted, the author and the publisher make no explicit guarantees as to the accuracy of the information included in this book and, in some cases, the names of people, places and organisations may have been altered to protect their privacy. All hyperlinks were believed to be live and correctly detailed at the time of publication.

This book may include references to organisations, feature films, television programmes, popular songs, musical bands, novels, reference books, and other creative works, the titles of which are trademarks and/or registered trademarks, and which are the intellectual properties of their respective copyright holders.

All rights reserved. No part of this publication may be reproduced, stored in a retrieval system, or transmitted, in any form or by any means, electronic, mechanical, photocopying, recording or otherwise, without the prior permission in writing of the publisher.

This book is sold subject to the condition that it shall not, by way of trade or otherwise, be lent, re-sold or hired out, or otherwise circulated without the publisher's prior consent in any form of binding or cover other than that in which it is published and without a similar condition including this condition being imposed on the subsequent purchaser.

A CIP catalogue record for this book is available from the British Library.

ISBN: 978-1-7394845-9-0

Typeset in Sorts Mill Goudy, designed by The League of Moveable Type.

Printed and bound in Great Britain by IngramSpark, Chapter House, Pitfield, Kiln Farm, Milton Keynes, MK11 3LW, United Kingdom.

Cover artwork is Copyright © Natalie Hora at Shutterstock, all rights reserved.

Cover design and book design is Copyright © Thomas A. Christie.

Author images are Copyright © Murray Cook, all rights reserved.

Internal photographic images are Copyright © Murray Cook, and are sourced from the author's private collection unless otherwise stated in the Image Credits section, which forms an extension to this legal page.

The copyrights of third parties are reserved. All third party imagery is used under the provision of Fair Use for the purposes of commentary and criticism. While every reasonable effort has been made to contact copyright holders and secure permission for all images reproduced in this work, we offer apologies for any instances in which this was not possible and for any inadvertent omissions.

Contents

Introduction .... Page i
Map of Stirling City .... Page vi
Map of Stirling and Environs .... Page viii

Hidden Stirling .... Page 1

Acknowledgements .... Page 100
Endnotes .... Page 101
Image Credits .... Page 102
About the Author .... Page 107

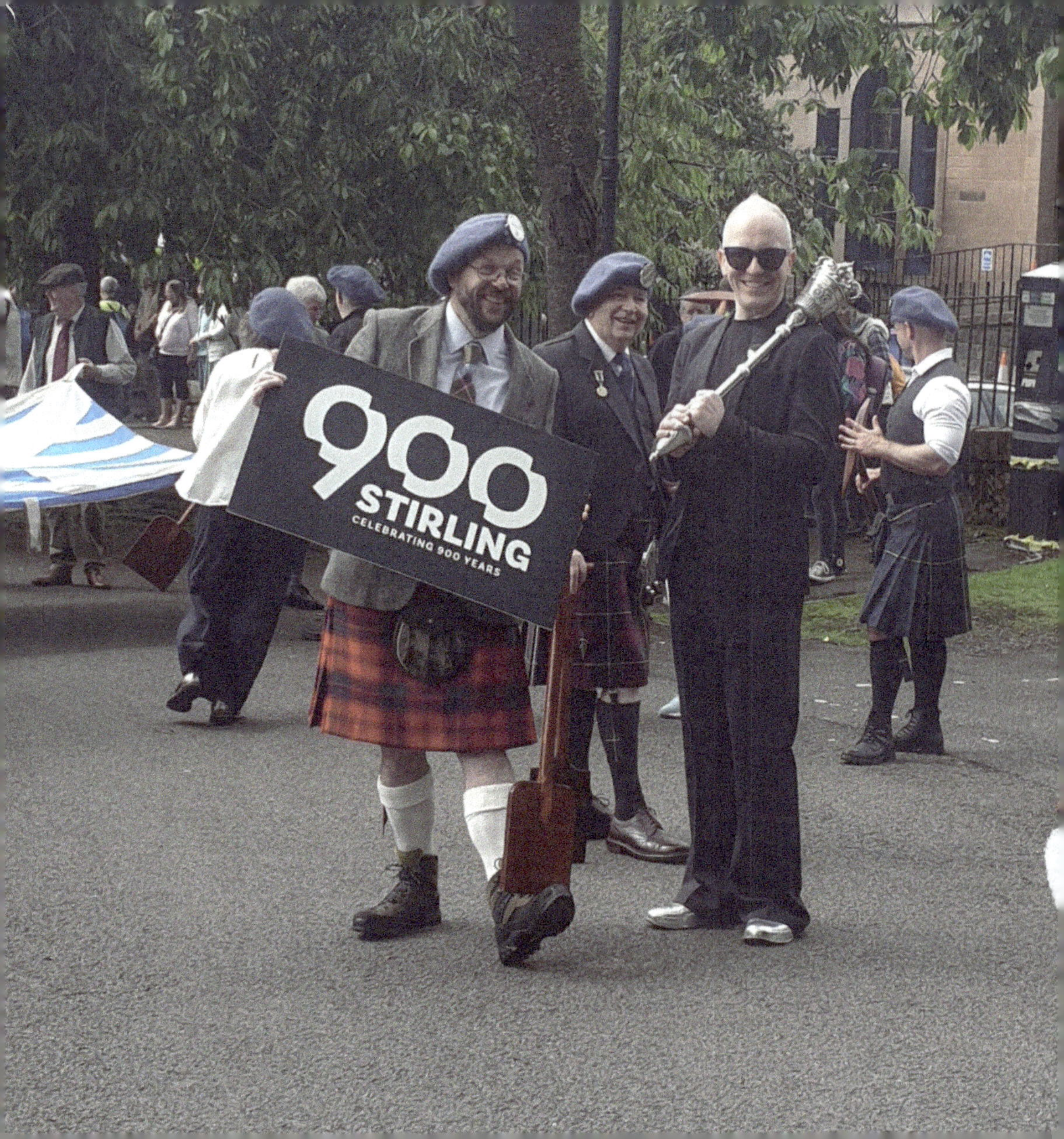
900
STIRLING
CELEBRATING 900 YEARS

Introduction

Stirling, Scotland's smallest city, packs a big punch. We think the burgh (as it was known) was founded in 1124—and, as I write this book, it's just celebrated its 900th birthday![1] It was clawed from the Kingdom of Northumbria, and it took a few hundred years for the Sons and Daughters of the Rock to consider themselves actually Scottish. Because of our frontier location on the River Forth, anyone who wished to invade or resist that invasion did it at Stirling: *the brooch that holds together the two parts of the country.*

This small and hopefully fun book is about 50 wee nooks and crannies most locals have missed or can't get access to. Some are hidden, others locked, stolen, demolished or extinct—some were even declared illegal, and one never even existed! It's mostly about Stirling, but I've put a few gems from beyond our boundaries—even as far as Falkirk! I've provided locations for each of the sites (or as for close as you can or are allowed to get!).

The book is based on my nosey interests (I am proud to be Stirling Council's Archaeologist), and I can't resist a closed door or a hidden passage. I hope you enjoy it. It's organised geographically, and each location has a grid reference. Sometimes the sites are in clusters and—if you want to walk them—I've organised them in an appropriate order. They are also numbered and linked to the maps.

A note on access: in Scotland, we enjoy the Right to Roam, which means you can go anywhere that isn't inside a building or a private garden. If in doubt, ask and please always keep dogs on leashes, leave gates as you find them, don't walk through crops, and take your litter with you. You are welcome here, but please don't embarrass me.

HIDDEN STIRLING

Murray Cook

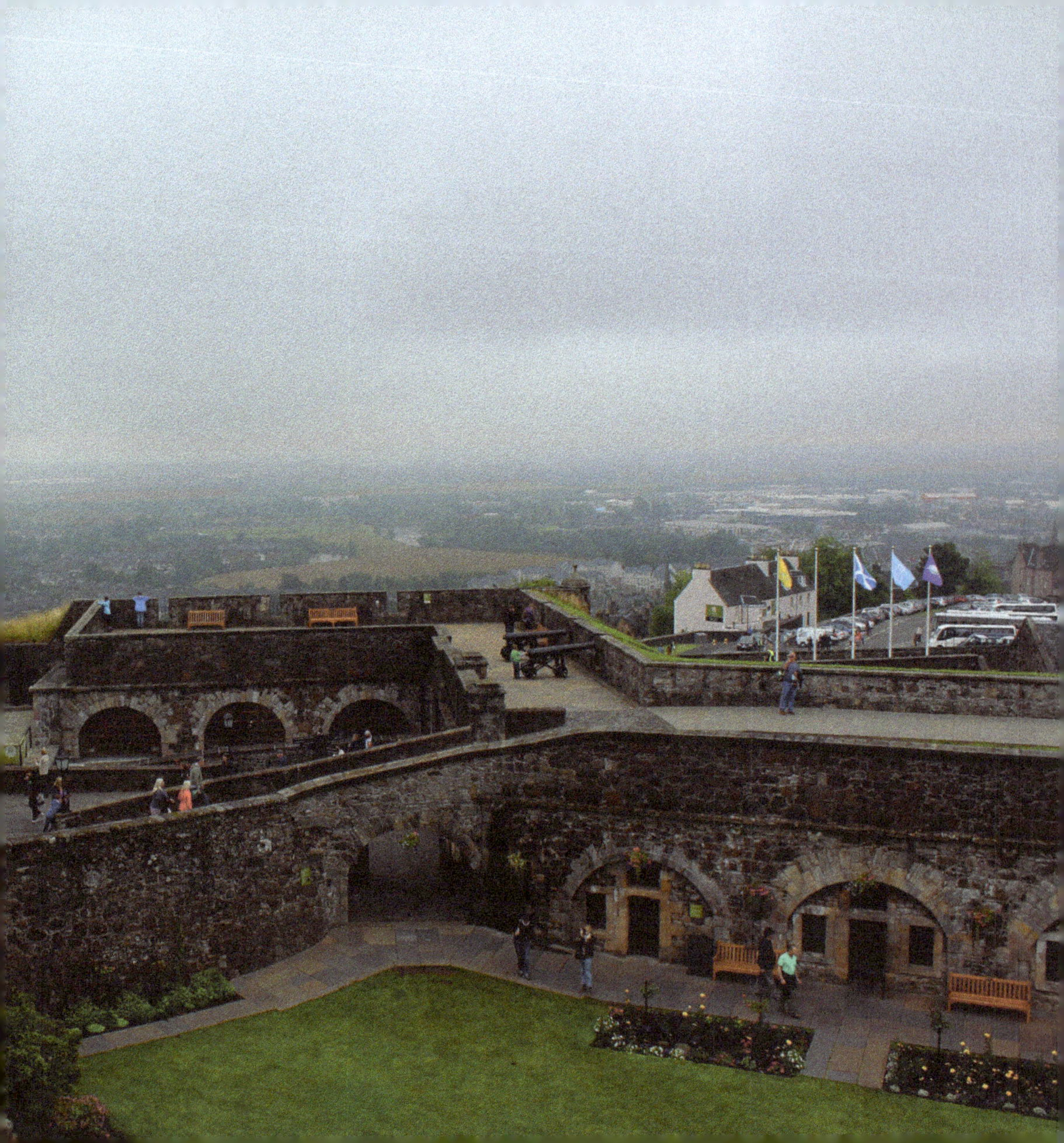

This book is dedicated to my brothers Martin and Graeme who, despite our various ups and downs, have always had my back.

vi

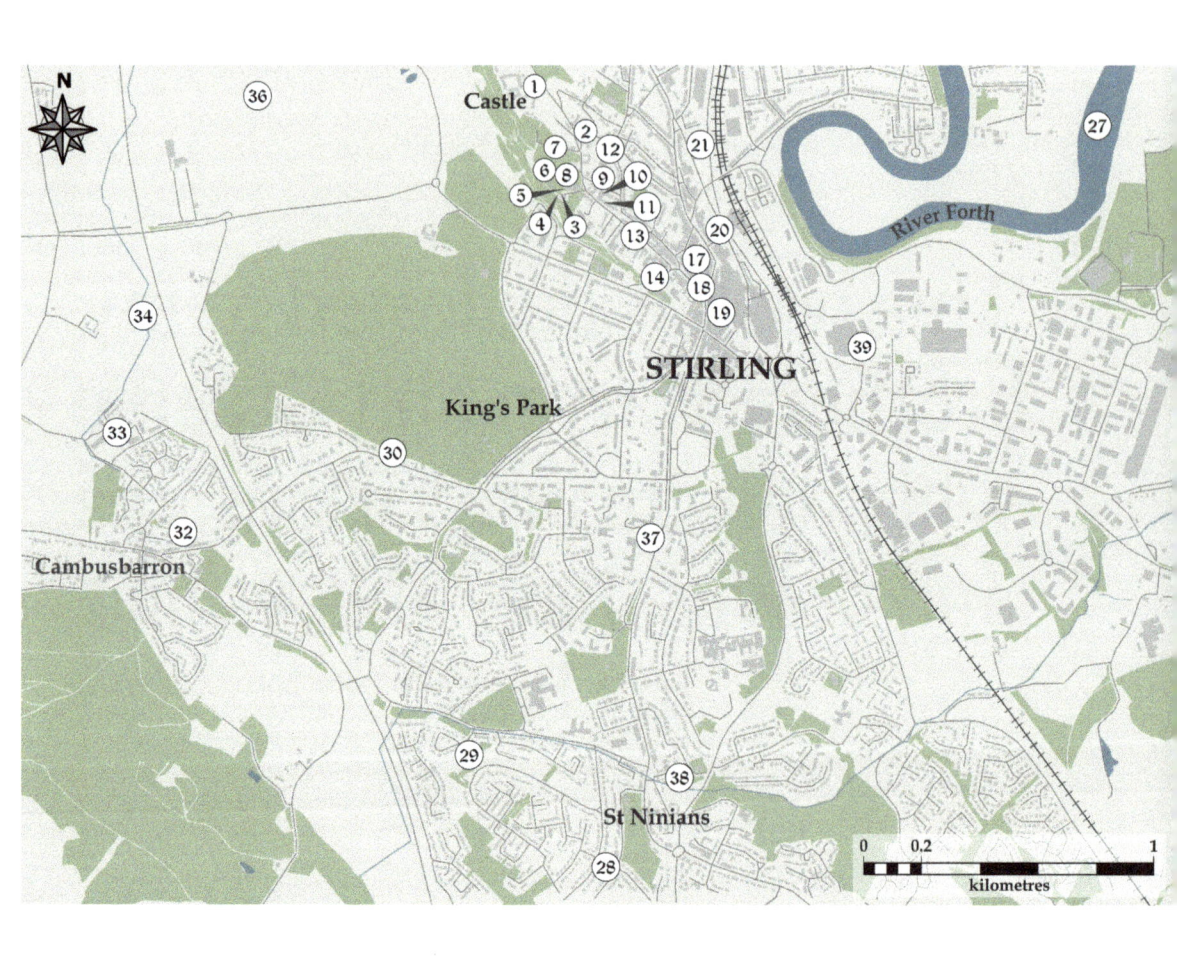

Map of Stirling City

KEY:

1. The Guidman o' Ballangeich
2. Bare and Empty
3. Secrets of the Cemetery 1
4. Secrets of the Cemetery 2
5. Secrets of the Cemetery 3
6. Secrets of the Cemetery 4
7. Secrets of the Cemetery 5
8. Secrets of the Cemetery 6
9. Tea for Two Pavilions?
10. Stirling Tolbooth
11. Killing is Our Business
12. John Cowane's Honey
13. David I
14. Secrets of the Municipal Building 1
17. Skeletons and Axes
18. Mr Burns Gets into Trouble
19. Stirling's Buried Street
20. Warring Bedfellows
21. The Stank at the Provost's Pool
27. The Most Important Ford in Scotland
28. Homes for Heroes
29. The Road to Destiny
30. A Lost Cemetery
34. The Oldest Functioning Lade
36. The Ten Aces from Raploch
37. Stirling's Oldest War Memorial?
38. St Ninians Tower
39. Clock Watching for 132 Years and Counting!

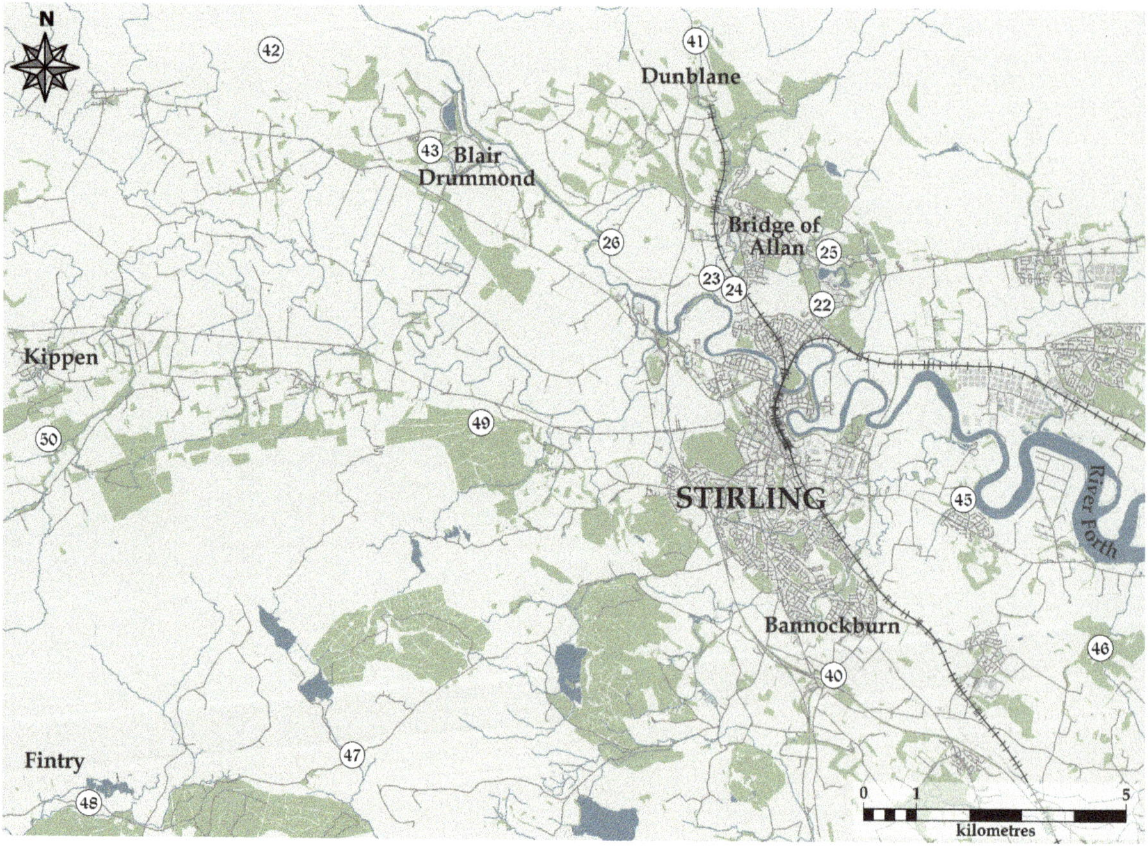
N
42
41
Dunblane
43
Blair
Drummond
Bridge of
Allan
25
26
23
24
22
Kippen
49
50
STIRLING
45
River Forth
Bannockburn
46
40
47
Fintry
48
0
1
5
kilometres

Map of Stirling and Environs

KEY:

- 22   William Wallace's Real HQ
- 23   Bridge of Allan-on-Sea
- 24   Robert Louis Stevenson
- 25   The Hermit of Bridge of Allan
- 26   Collected to Extinction
- 40   From Top to Bottom
- 41   By Royal Appointment... Not!
- 42   Scotland's Heart
- 43   Christ's Well
- 45   An Abandoned Freezer in Fallin!
- 46   Winding Up the Age of Improvement
- 47   Lost and Forgotten Frontiers and a Camel!
- 48   The Gowk's Stanes
- 49   Another Lost Cemetery
- 50   An Illegal Church and a Minister on the Run!

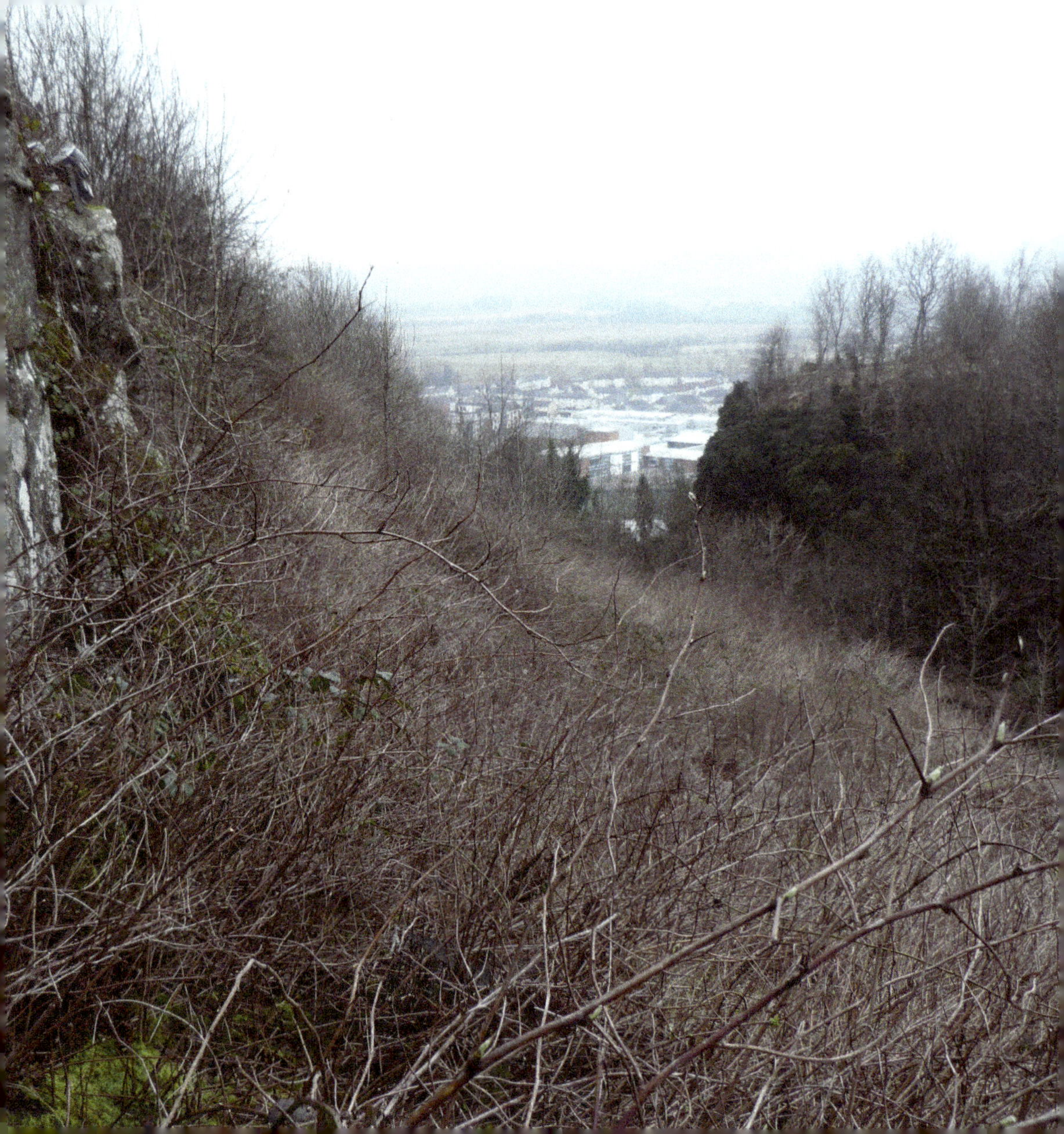

The Guidman o' Ballengeich

So, have you been one of the 600,000 tourists who annually storm Stirling Castle, one of the best preserved Renaissance Palaces in Europe? Built from the smoking ashes after Robert the Bruce—fresh from his greatest victory at the Battle of Bannockburn—destroyed it. Scotland was not yet free, and so he could not risk it falling into English hands again. Over time, James III, IV, V and VI all transformed the Castle into a suitable place to crown James V and Mary Queen of Scots—though really this was not a badge of pride but of failure; Scotland was too unstable to risk these child monarchs outside Stirling's high walls.

However, what I wanted to say was that when the Castle was at its peak, none of us would have been allowed to go in the main entrance. We would have had to go to the north of the Castle at Ballengeich Road; a name which is clearly Gaelic in origin. *Bal-* tends to mean village, but in this case the name is often interpreted as 'windy pass'. Famously, James V was known as 'The Guidman o' Ballengeich', because—according to legend—he used a small track down to Ballengeich Road to have various adventures in disguise amongst his subjects.

Later quarrying lowered the road and made the bank steeper (and it's now covered in brambles), and the gate was blocked in 1689. However, the remains of the Sally Port—which was designed to be used to send small numbers of troops out during an attack—survive. These are marked on the inside by a wee sign, though nothing connects it to James V or the hundreds of anonymous people over the centuries that trudged this way to do their business in the castle. But I went that way, so you don't have to!

NS 79072 94060

Bare and Empty
The Reformation's Impact on Stirling

Stirling's second oldest building is the Church of the Holy Rude[2] and, while it was founded in the 12th century, this current version dates mostly from the 15th or 16th century. Its battle-scarred walls have seen centuries of conflict and debate, and it is the only upstanding building in Scotland to have witnessed a coronation (James VI's). While magnificent, it is austere when it was once loud and celebratory; its walls were once lined with a clay mortar which should be bright and eye-catching. All of its splendour and riches were stripped away in the Reformation when Scotland transitioned from Catholicism to Protestantism. While this is not the place to debate what we gained and lost through this, it is worth noting that the Kirk banned Christmas in Scotland and it didn't become a Bank Holiday until the 20th century!

Anyway, to my mind the greatest losses were the various icons that commemorated saints as well as Christ and Mary. Around the Church of the Holy Rude's eastern end are eleven empty niches that once held richly decorated icons that, to Protestants, were sinful and had to go. All of the niches are slightly different, and while a lot of the detail has gone it's clear that one has a saltire, while another (pictured) has a grotesque... a little monstrous little face, gurning for eternity. Is it my imagination, or is he howling in outrage at the loss of his icon?

These next seven stories are organised in a loop round the Top o' The Town, past the church and into and around the cemetery: the dead centre of Stirling. I recommend you walk around the bottom of the castle and past the Portcullis hotel, which is a good place for lunch. In tourist season the café at Cowane's Hospital is great for coffee, soup and buns!

NS 79236 93709

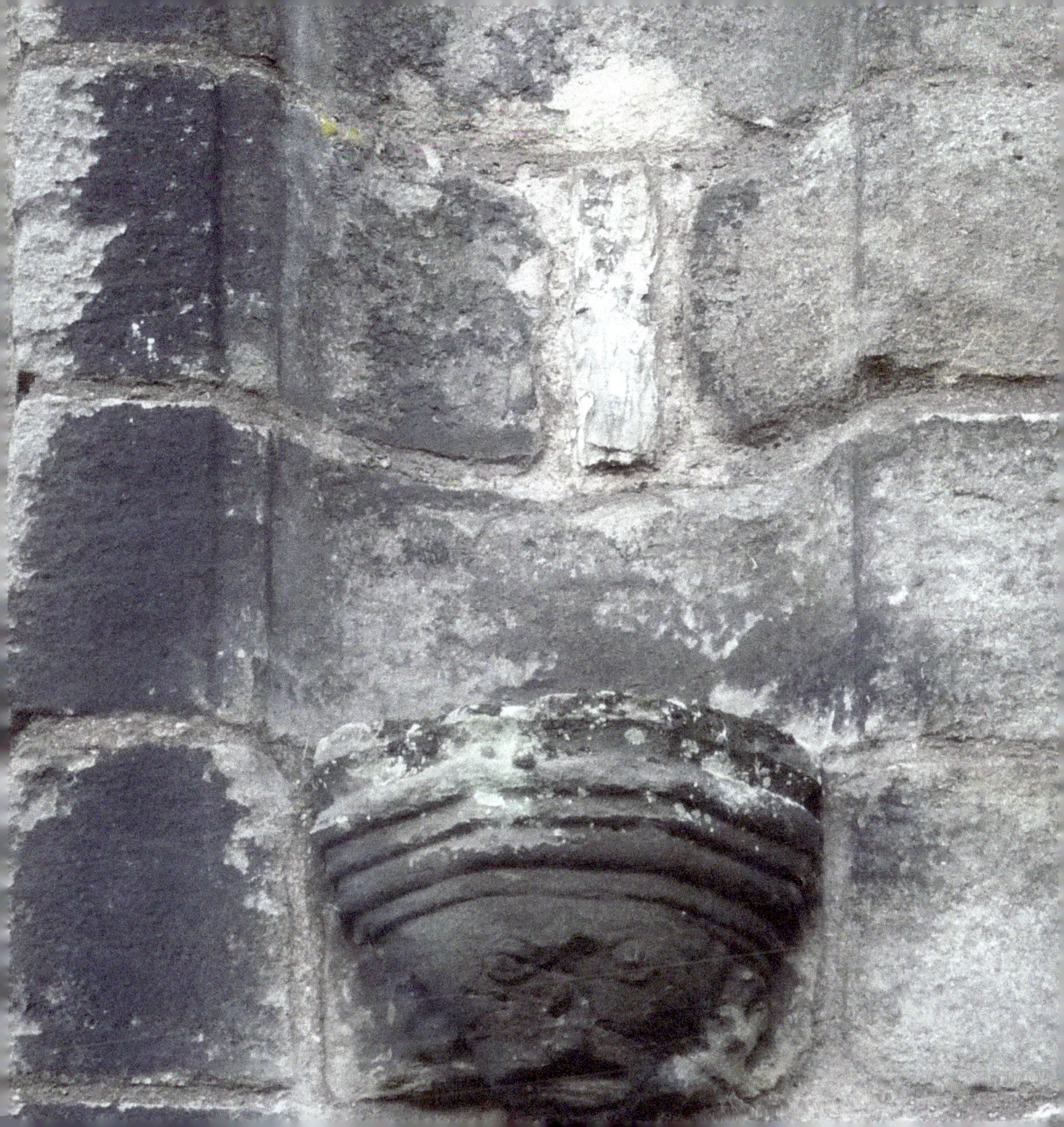

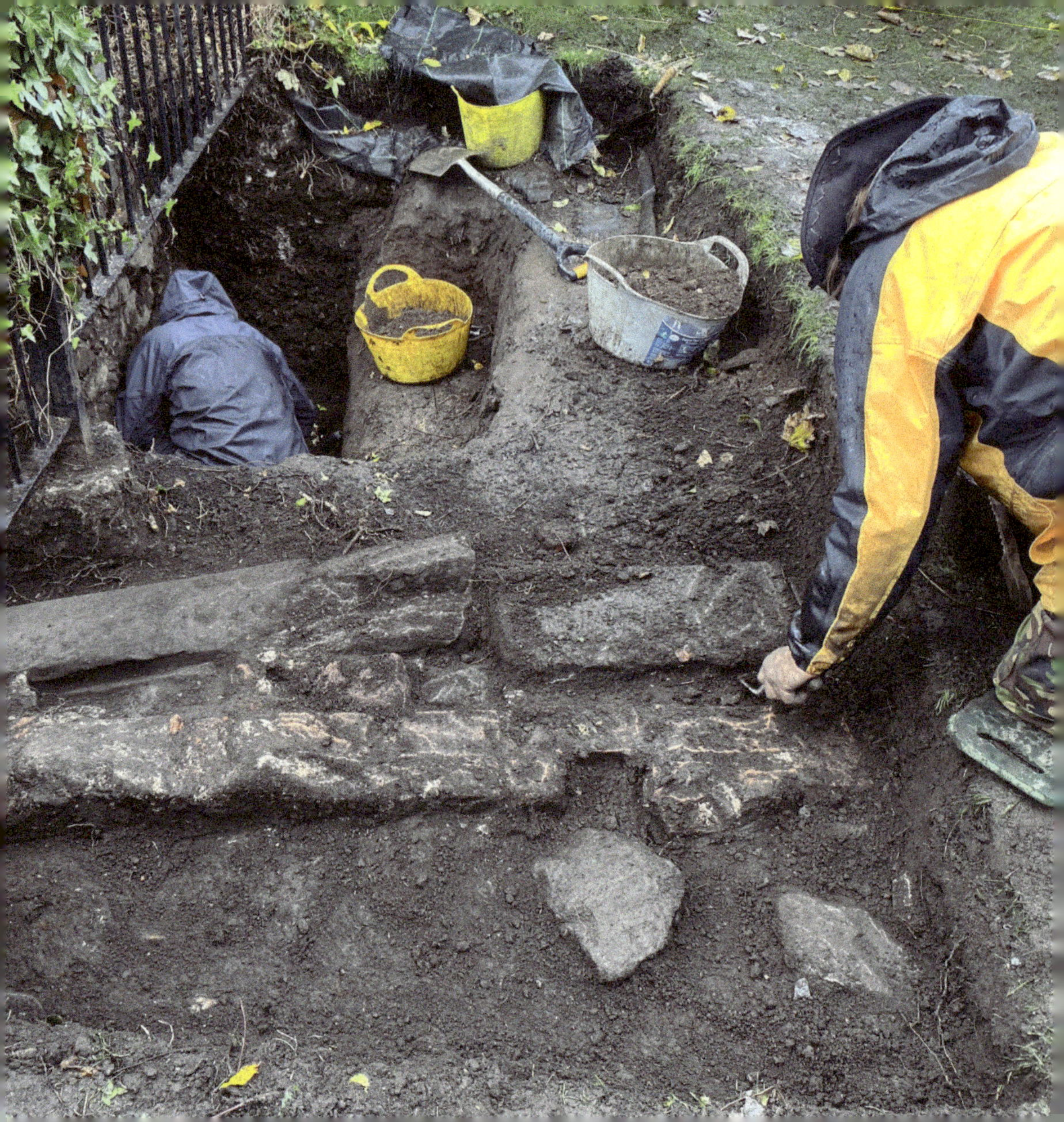

Secrets of the Cemetery 1

A Cold Lonely, Sleepless Vigil Deterring Grave Robbers

Everyone knows about Edinburgh's most famous serial killers: Burke and Hare. They progressed from grave robbing to murder to supply trainee doctors with fresh corpses for dissection. Stirling's most infamous grave-robbing incident involved Mary Stevenson[3] who was buried in the Old Town Cemetery on 16th November 1822... but not for long. Her corpse was stolen on behalf of Dr John Forrest. Though the robbers were caught, the subsequent trial was botched and Forrest escaped. There was a riot in response, and troops were called from the Castle to suppress the crowd—though shots were fired, there were no serious injuries. Eventually Forrest received a royal pardon, joined the military and became honorary physician to Queen Victoria! The fate of poor Mary remains unknown, as she was never recovered. Grave-robbing was stopped by the 1832 Anatomy Act, which regulated the bodies of freshly executed criminals. Today people have to volunteer to help students and, when my time comes, I've already signed up.

However, before the practice was stopped, grieving relatives attempted various ways to prevent robbers digging up their loved ones. Sometimes an iron grill, or 'mort safe', was placed over the grave. A cheaper option was to employ a guard in the cemetery and keep watch, as you really only needed to do this for a few days while nature took its course. I cannot think of anything more miserable than such a cold lonely, sleepless vigil. After Mary's case, a guard house was built in the south-east corner of the cemetery to house those standing watch. This was cleared in the middle of the 19th century when the cemetery's walls were lowered. The picture is from our excavation of the site and shows its foundation. Ironically, it's clear that the building's construction involved the removal of several graves!

This point is immediately to the left of the main cemetery entrance at the Church of The Holy Rude; look for the place with no headstones.

NS 79159 93689

Secrets of the Cemetery 2
Stirling's Last Line of Defence

At the time of writing this (May 2024), the war in Ukraine was still grinding on and it brought to mind our own city defences. These, the best preserved city walls in Scotland, are of course just pleasant, peaceful tourist attractions now. My daughters played in the shadow of the bastion in Allan's Primary school, its cannon long gone. Stirling's walls were built in the middle of the 16th century to defend Stirling against an attack by Henry VIII's troops. He wanted to force the infant Mary, Queen of Scots to marry his young son Prince Edward (the Rough Wooing), but they were also used against Cromwell and Bonnie Prince Charlie's troops. This location is at the newest-discovered element of the wall, a position of strength (a bastion) to protect Stirling's last surviving medieval gate.

Centuries of peace, union and democracy between Scotland and England ensured that the walls became a relict and an ever number of greater and larger holes were burst through them as the burgh's roads expanded. But, unlike Edinburgh, Stirling's growth never lapped up and spilled out over the walls. Indeed until the start of the 19th century Stirling was more or less the same size it had been since James IV was on the throne. Peace brought trade and expansion and when the houses of Kings Park were built the area became a parkland, almost a boulevard with impressive public buildings: The Smith Museum, the Albert Halls and two churches, as well as space for statues and war memorials. All of it an absolutely wonderful example of late Victorian and Edwardian urban design; one of the best in Scotland. But in amongst all of this, the wall stands frozen—a memory of more troubled times—and you can still find spots where soldiers, all with a mixture of fear and bravery, stood with their guns on the lookout for invaders. My thoughts and prayers are with the brave Ukrainians.

Walk west along the fence for 10 paces and on your left is the footings of the Bastion.

NS 79148 93695

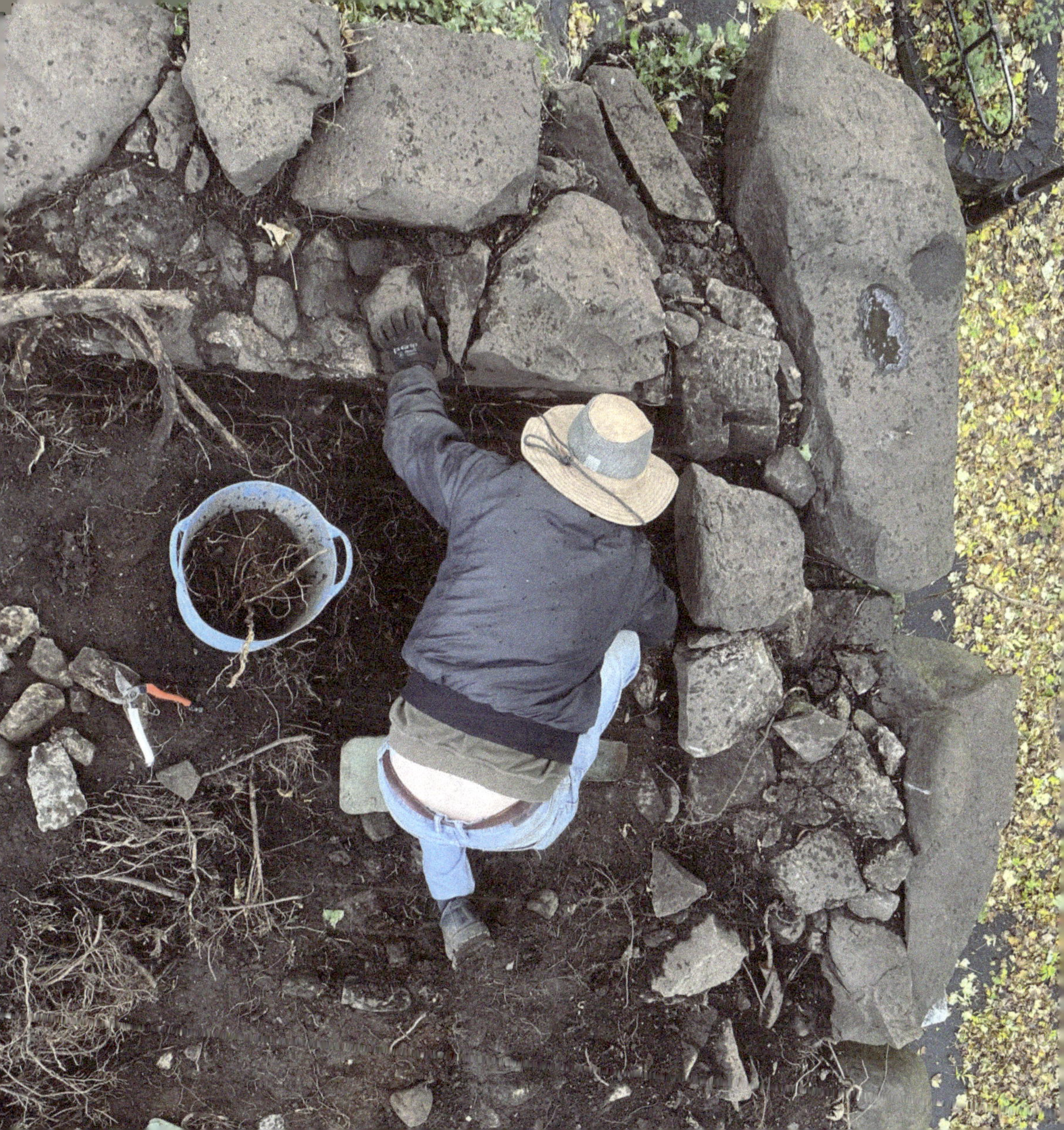

Mibiri Creek, Demerara River.
Mr. Edmonston's Wood Cutting Establishment.

Secrets of the Cemetery 3
The Banality of Evil

Famously, during the trial of the Nazi Adolph Eichmann, the phrase 'the banality of evil' was coined by Hannah Arendt: how could such a bland individual be responsible for such atrocities? Thankfully, very few of us are ever confronted with such systematic industrial evil as the Holocaust. We live—for the most part—safe, quiet, private lives, just like the Edmonstones. Their family memorial in the Top o' The Town cemetery is a modest, understated account of tragedy. Life was very hard before modern medicine, and several of their children died before their parents.

You will have spotted a few exotic locations: Trinidad and Demerara—the latter now part of Guyana in South America, and of course famous for its sugar. The hard work on these plantations was undertaken by slaves from Africa, captured for European profit. Sugar plantations were the Edmonstone family business. From their comfortable Georgian mansion in Melville Place, father and sons directed and oversaw industrial-scale evil. Famously, Europeans faced a very high mortality rate in the region due to tropical diseases and the harsh environment; hence the Edmonstone family deaths in Guyana and Trinidad. However, the death rate of the poor enslaved Africans was far higher—perhaps 1 in 15 in a good year, which doubled in a bad year. These trafficked and enslaved people faced the same conditions that killed the Europeans, without any of the benefits of wealth and freedom: they were confused, chained and beaten (the women suffered worse fates), given new names, and they died in their droves. When these poor people resisted, as in the Demerara Rebellion of 1823—a largely non-violent protest—they were brutally crushed and killed; a violent suppression in which the Edmonstones played a role. Once 'order' was restored, the bodies of those slaves viewed as the ringleaders of the protest were hung in chains on the public roads and left to rot. How could such an apparently normal Stirling family be responsible for such atrocities?

With the bastion behind you walk in a perpendicular line with the church of your right for around 10–20 paces.

NS 79164 93708

Secrets of the Cemetery 4
The Syphilis Doctor

In the very western corner of the cemetery lies a hidden and overlooked grave; you have to walk around it to find the life it celebrates. It lies between two much grander graves, and a variety of smaller ones. The one to the right is to Stirling's first publisher, while to the left is the Smith family who ran Hayford Mills, and about whom we will hear more later on. Now, the reason that this grave is overlooked is not because of some dark shame borne by the inhabitant; he lived a useful and virtuous life. Rather, it is simply that new memorials have sprung up around him and his final resting place.

The individual in question, Dr Abraham Gordon, was a Royal Navy Surgeon who had an illustrious career and died in his eighties. He was serving during the Jacobite '45 Rising, though his thoughts on the whole affair are not recorded. Of course, in January 1746 the cemetery was the scene of an exchange of cannon fire from Jacobites attempting the last ever siege of Stirling castle—it failed. Returning to the good Doctor, his chief claim to fame is to have developed one of the first treatments for syphilis in the British military!

With the church behind you, walk towards the west end of the cemetery with Ladies Rock to your right.

NS 79104 93753

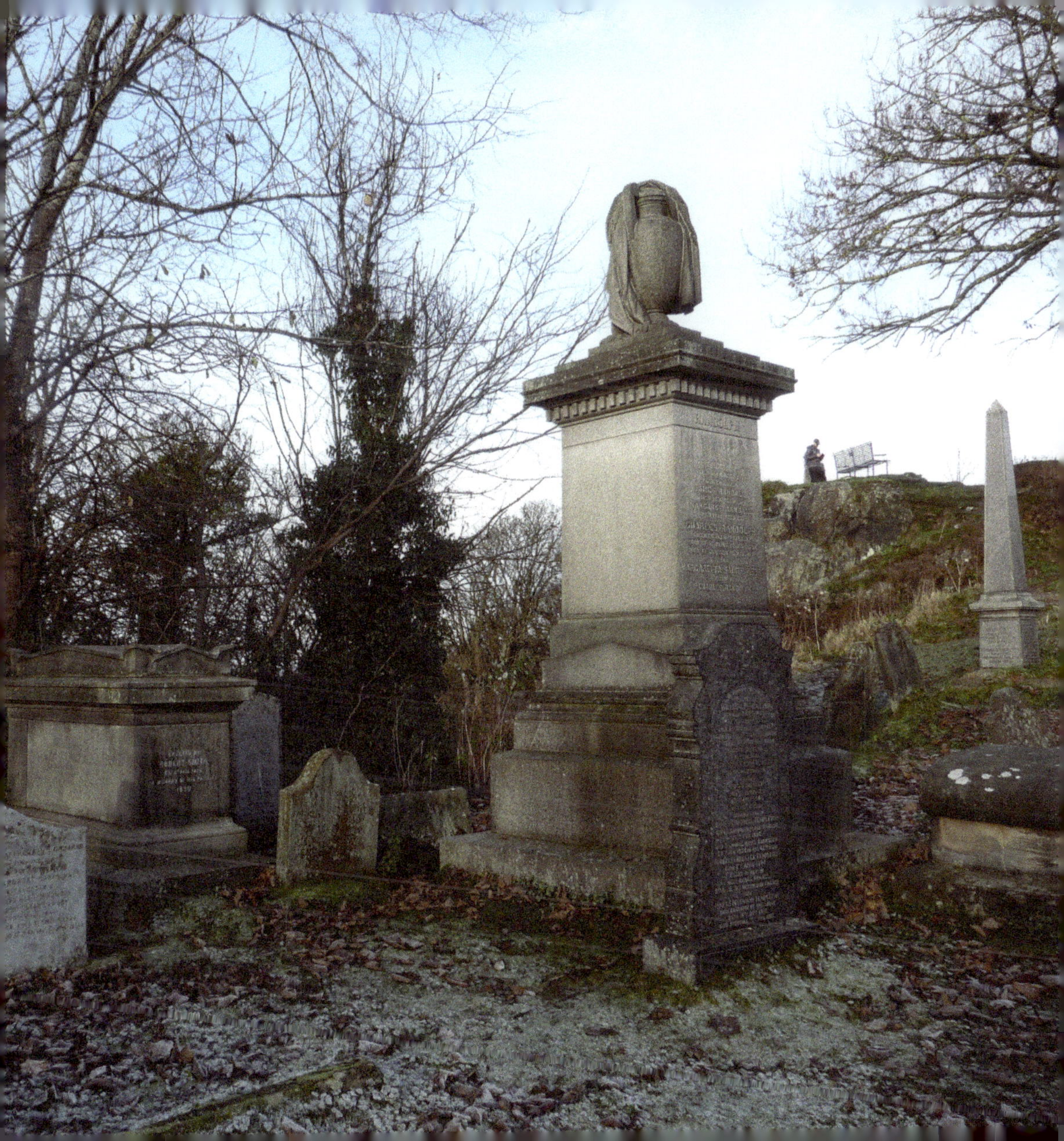

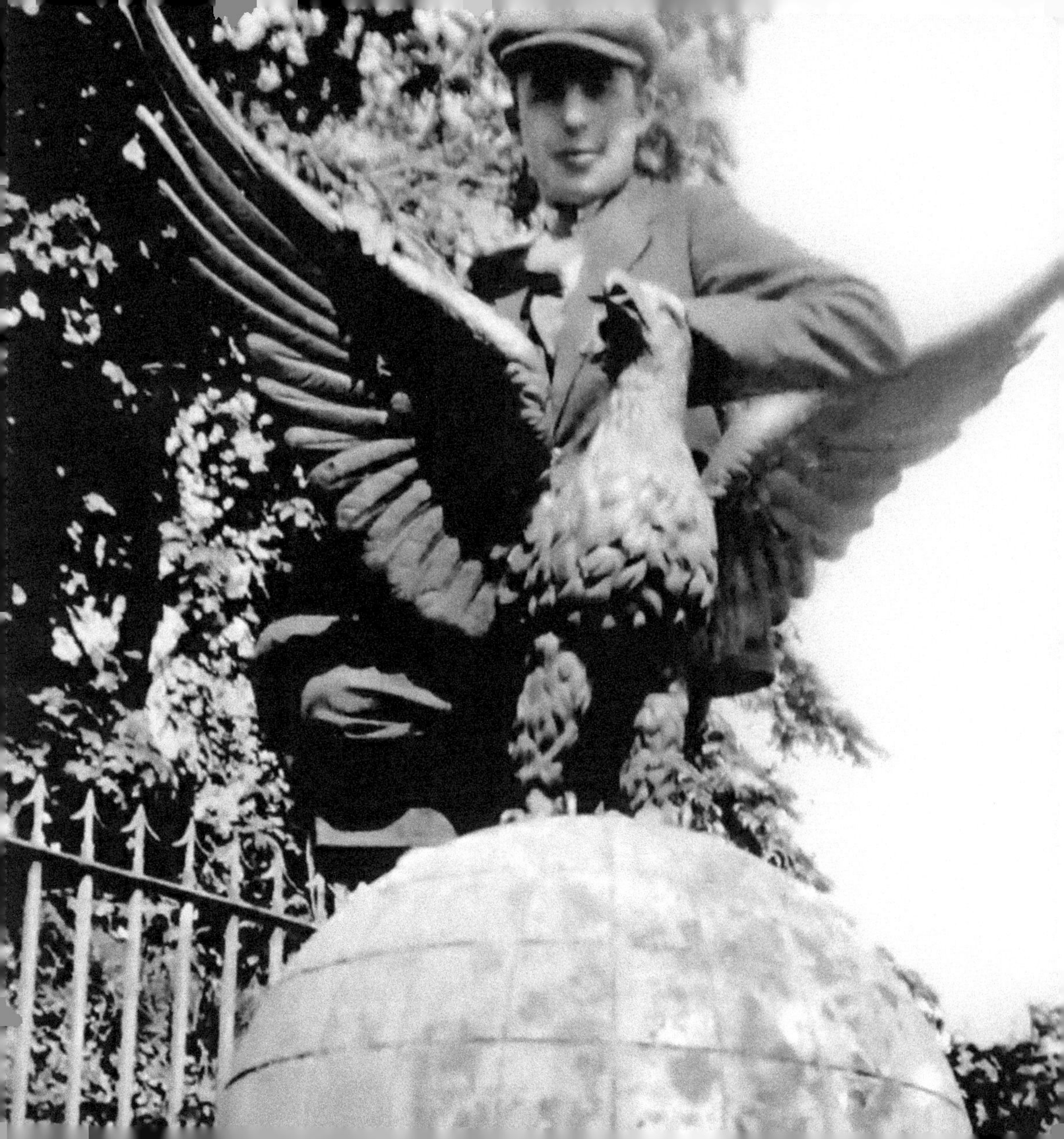

Secrets of the Cemetery 5
The Flight of Stirling's Bronze Eagles

The complex of cemeteries between Stirling Castle and the Church of the Holy Rude is a wonderful place with vast panoramic views. The poet William Wordsworth said 'we know of no sweeter cemetery in all of our wanderings than that of Stirling'. It drips with history and conflict. It witnessed Mary, Queen of Scots' celebration of the baptism of her son: the future James VI, who would commission the King James Bible. As we've heard, Bonnie Prince Charlie tried and failed to capture the castle in its last ever siege during January 1746. In 1651, Cromwell's troops had a fire-fight between the stones. It has seen witch executions and grave robbing, and the stones feature Celtic Crosses and Green Men.

Looming above them all is one of Scotland's largest pyramids. Known as the Star Pyramid, or Salem Rock, it was commissioned in 1863 by William Drummond, a wealthy evangelical Christian. William himself is buried in a prominent polished granite tomb to the side. The monument has bibles around its base and, like the rest of the Valley Cemetery with its various statues, is a monument to the leaders and martyrs of the Church of Scotland, of people who fought and died for religious and political freedom. The intention was to provide not just a pleasant garden but something edifying for the working classes to aspire to: a great British Empire straddling the world, white and protestant. At the base of the Pyramid were two large bronze eagles sitting on top of globes; a favourite place for people to sit on. The cemetery fell into disrepair after the 1960s and was subject to repeated vandalism, including inscriptions on grave stones (disgusting) and metal theft, and at some point the eagles took flight and have never been seen since!

Turn around and head to the big pyramid!

NS 79145 93849

Secrets of the Cemetery 6
Major Arthur Forbes: from Argyll to the Battle of Moore's Creek Bridge, Wilmington, North Carolina?

Arthur Forbes was born after the Jacobite 1745 Rising, on the shores of Loch Fyne, and went on to become a Major in His Majesty's North Carolina Highlanders. Now, as many of you will know, this regiment consisted of Gaelic-speaking volunteers, many of them ex-Jacobites, who had settled in the US, but would rather fight for a king (any king) than a republic! According to tradition, the North Carolina Highlanders were formed from Royalist volunteers determined to oppose the American Revolution. Famously, ahead of their first fight they were addressed in Gaelic by Flora MacDonald, who had left Scotland for America after helping Bonnie Prince Charlie escape in the wake of the Jacobite 1745 Rising.

The loyalists famously attempted a ferocious Highland Charge at the Revolutionary position on Moore's Creek Bridge at dawn on 27th February 1776. This involved running at defensive positions while firing all your guns; in theory, you scared your opposition and hit them before they could reload. Unfortunately, they were completely defeated, and many were captured. After the battle, many refused to fight for either side and—after the war—several were chased north into Canada. One Revolutionary Sergeant, Donald MacDonald, whose father had fought with Bonnie Prince Charlie and for the King at Moore's Creek, lamented at what he saw in his father's generation's betrayal of their American friends. To add insult to injury, the British Crown refused to compensate the Gaels for the loss of the American lands, which were confiscated by Congress. Flora always said in her later life that she first served the House of Stuart and then the House of Hanover, and that she was worsted in the cause of each.

At present, we don't precisely know if Arthur fought at Moore's Creek but it seems likely. After the end of the war he married and his children fought, settled and died across the rest of the British Empire: New South Wales, Canada and Burma!

From the pyramid, head back towards the church to its north side.

NS 79184 93736

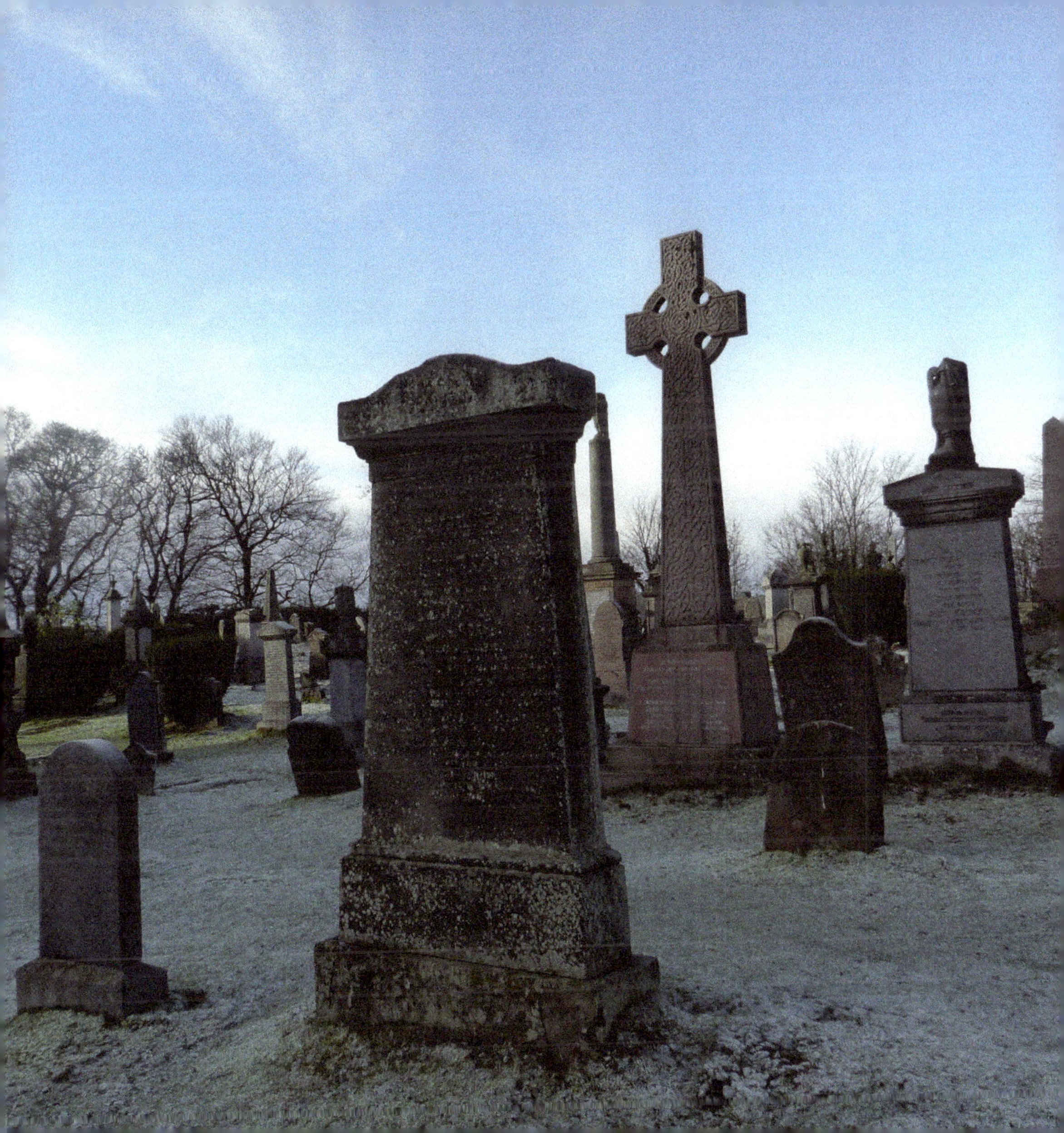

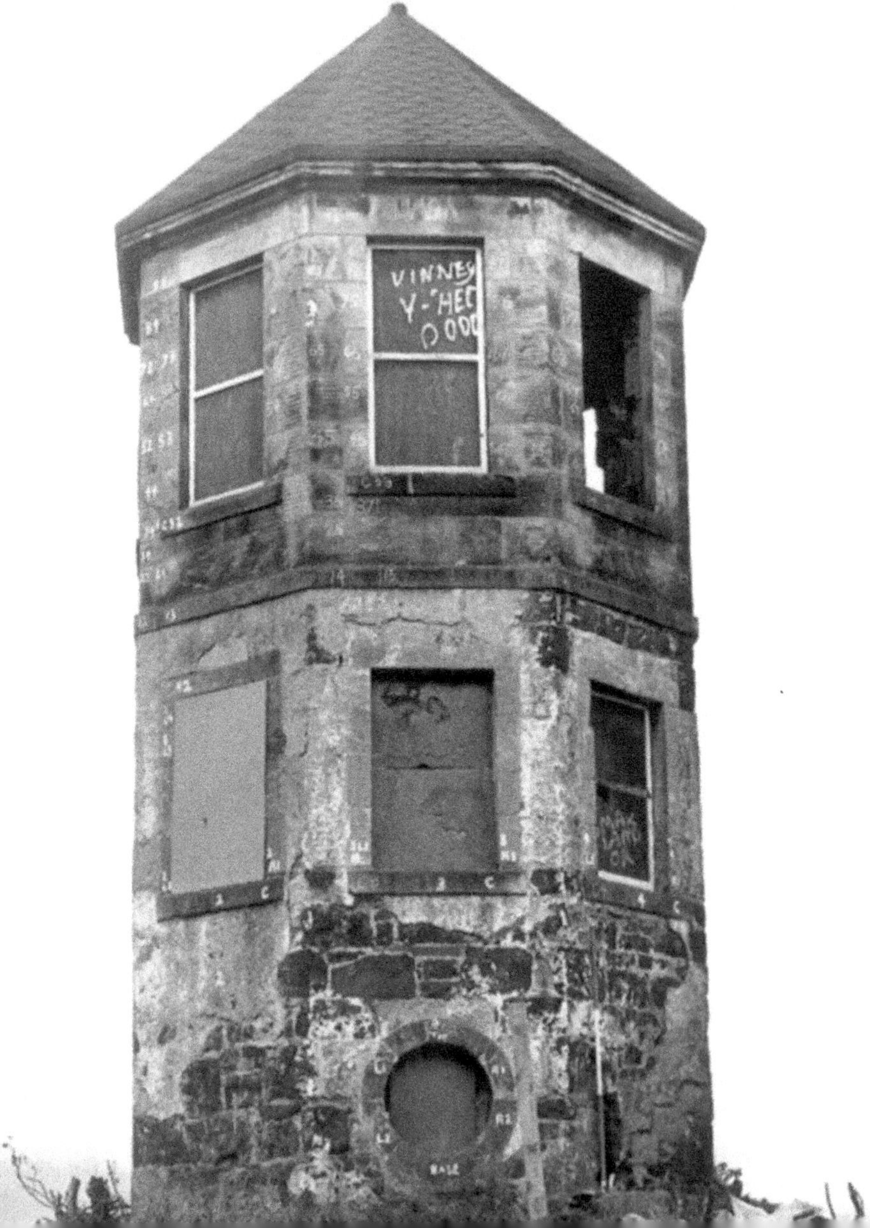

Tea for Two Pavilions?

Nineteenth century Stirling was a very fashionable and prosperous place; perhaps one of the richest places in the world. The twin pillars of Empire flowed through the city: commerce and the military. The Castle was a barracks and, as well as serving soldiers, Stirling was full of retired officers who had fought or explored every corner of the world. This was aided by rich Glasgow merchants commuting in and out of the city: the Empire's Second City.

The trend-conscious citizens spared no expenses, from elaborate plaster work interiors to vast quantities of decorative iron work outside—most of which was removed during World War II. For those that could afford it, the ultimate status symbol was a garden tea pavilion. Now, we know that today's elite have all sorts in their garden, but none of these are tea pavilions, which are sometime called observatories. These are narrow stone towers, perhaps two or three stories high, designed to provide 360 degree views. The space was so small that the staircases were outside the structure. There are two rare surviving examples in Stirling, both in a sorry state. The first is located in the grounds of the Hollybank restaurant (though watch out, it's a dangerous building (NS 79700 90990)), and the second (pictured) is in an even worse state. It was far more impressive and located to the north of Broad Street (where you are!) with what must have been incredible views to The Ochils. It is owned by Stirling Council and was carefully numbered, dismantled, and safely stored to be reconstructed at a later date. Unfortunately, it lies there still, sealed in a roofless building with its doors and windows bricked up: a slumbering, entombed giant from a lost and more prosperous Stirling, now forgotten and hidden.

The building is in the grounds of the Hollybank, though please don't try to access it.

NS 79297 93731

Stirling Tolbooth

From Witch Trials to Britain's Last Beheading

In Scotland, Tolbooths were where the Council and the Courts met and, while they had prison cells, these were where you waited before you were given a punishment—normally a physical one.

The current building was built around 1705, replacing an older medieval one which had had witnessed Stirling's largest ever witch trial in March 1659. This trial had resulted in the execution of Bessie Stevenson (perhaps an ancestor of Mary's?) who confessed to folk healing. This confession was of course made up; it is likely that she was tortured to make it, certainly cold, hungry and sleep deprived, and perhaps even 'pricked' to find a spot with no pain or no blood loss... the Devil's Spot. It is also possible that she may have been mentally ill. Regardless, she was found guilty of a crime that could not have taken place and Well Green, the scene of her 'crime', is still upstanding.

In 1820, the Tolbooth witnessed the trial and execution of Baird and Hardie, the leaders of the Radical War who were fighting for improved voting rights. They were found guilty of treason for which the punishment was beheading but, as the 19th century was a more enlightened age, this was commuted to hanging—and then the corpses were decapitated. The axe is on display in the Smith Art Gallery and Museum.

However, above all of this stands the tower, housing a lovely but very dusty bell. This was originally made in 1669 by Peter Hermony of Amsterdam. Unfortunately, it developed a crack and was recast in 1864 by John Wilson of Glasgow. Under this inscription sits our friend the Stirling Wolf and the Latin phrase meaning the City of Stirling. Just how many crimes and blighted lives has this bell seen...? I asked the wolf, but answer came there none.

While the Tolbooth's Bell Tower is not open to the public, the Tolbooth is a wonderful concert venue and the toilets nestle between prison cells... well worth a look!

NS 79310 93693

OPIDUM STERLINI

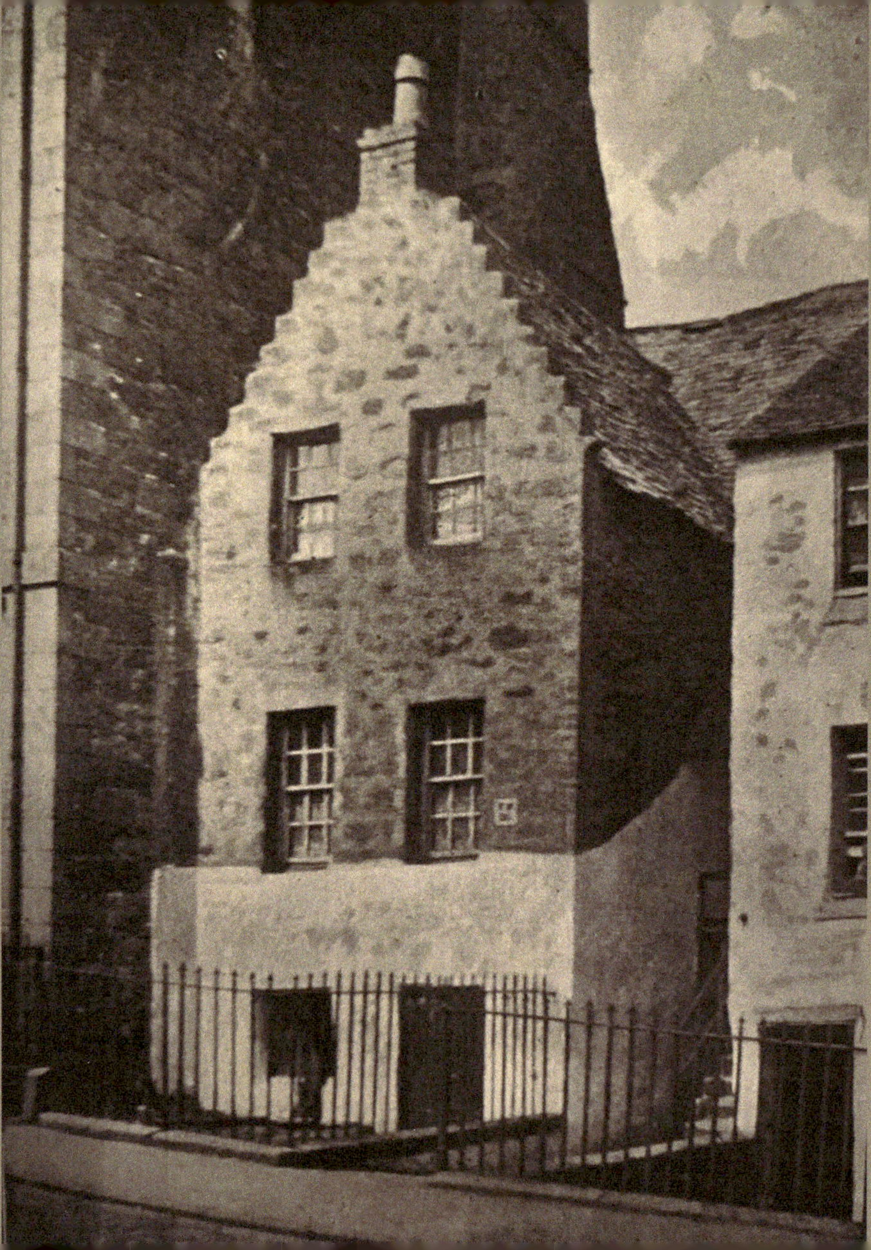

Killing is Our Business...

We just heard of Stirling's Tolbooth and how it kept prisoners while they awaited their punishments (which, as mentioned, tended to be physical). The man who enacted these sentences was called the Staffman, and his house was next to the Tolbooth and was known as the Hangman's House. Unfortunately it was demolished in the mid-20th century. The main gallows was just outside the medieval town, at a triangular garden now occupied by an ornate Victorian fountain with a cherub on top. The whole fountain was painted black and is known as the Black Boy Fountain. Legend has it that in order to avoid the jostling of the Stirling public, the Staffman had his own private entrance through the City Wall. However, he also undertook a number of other functions, including whipping people and, bizarrely, in 1734 publicly burning a 'false' book. Quite what was so terrible about this book is unrecorded, though it was probably a political manifesto!

However, on 8th September 1820, the Stirling mob was so angry that the Staffman wanted nothing to do with the scheduled execution. The 'criminals' were the aforementioned Baird and Hardie, who were subject to Britain's last beheading. So unpopular was their trial and execution that a different executioner had to be brought in from outside Stirling for a then-enormous fee of £20. The role was taken by one Mr Thomas Young, and even he had to wear a big cloak to hide his face. It was also unclear how one went about chopping someone's head off, and notes were exchanged between Stirling and Glasgow Burghs on the best approach. Finally, it's worth noting that Young died without having been paid for the execution, and there are letters in the archives from his widow asking for the £20!

As the Hangman's House has been demolished, this location is next to the close that gave access to his house, and where Baird and Hardie were executed.

NS 79319 93696

John Cowane's Honey

Have you heard of John Cowane, the 17th century merchant who left a fortune to Stirling? Well, his childhood home survives as a roofless ruin: a wonderful cluster of 16th century houses all crammed round together. It was once one of the grandest homes in Stirling; however, slowly but surely its status declined after the Union of the Crowns in 1603 when our Scottish James VI became England's James I. This meant that Stirling went from being from one of the most important places in Scotland to a backwater in Britain. Big houses ended up becoming flats, with far too many families crammed into far too small a space. Medieval water and drainage supplies could not cope and, by the end of the 19th century, Stirling had one of Scotland's lowest life expectancies and highest infant mortality rates. The building was saved from demolition by the trust that his will founded all of those centuries ago.

In its heyday, the Cowane family house had a large set of wonderful gardens, probably full of fruit trees and vegetable plots. Right at the back of the surviving garden are three small niches. These are bee boles, where hives were kept. These provided the family with a supply of very tasty honey. However, the apiculturists amongst you will have spotted a little issue. The boles are too close together for modern bees, who are more aggressive than their 16th century ancestors. Quite why this is the case, I have no idea, and I'm not sure if there is a moral to this story other than 'nothing ever stays the same'. But I will confess that my favourite part of any garden is something covered in 'bee loud' blossom, and that perhaps we all ought to do a bit more to keep them safe.

While the garden of Cowane's House is not open to the public, the front of the building which sits on the edge of the ancient burgh next to the King's stables is well worth a visit.

NS 79337 93843

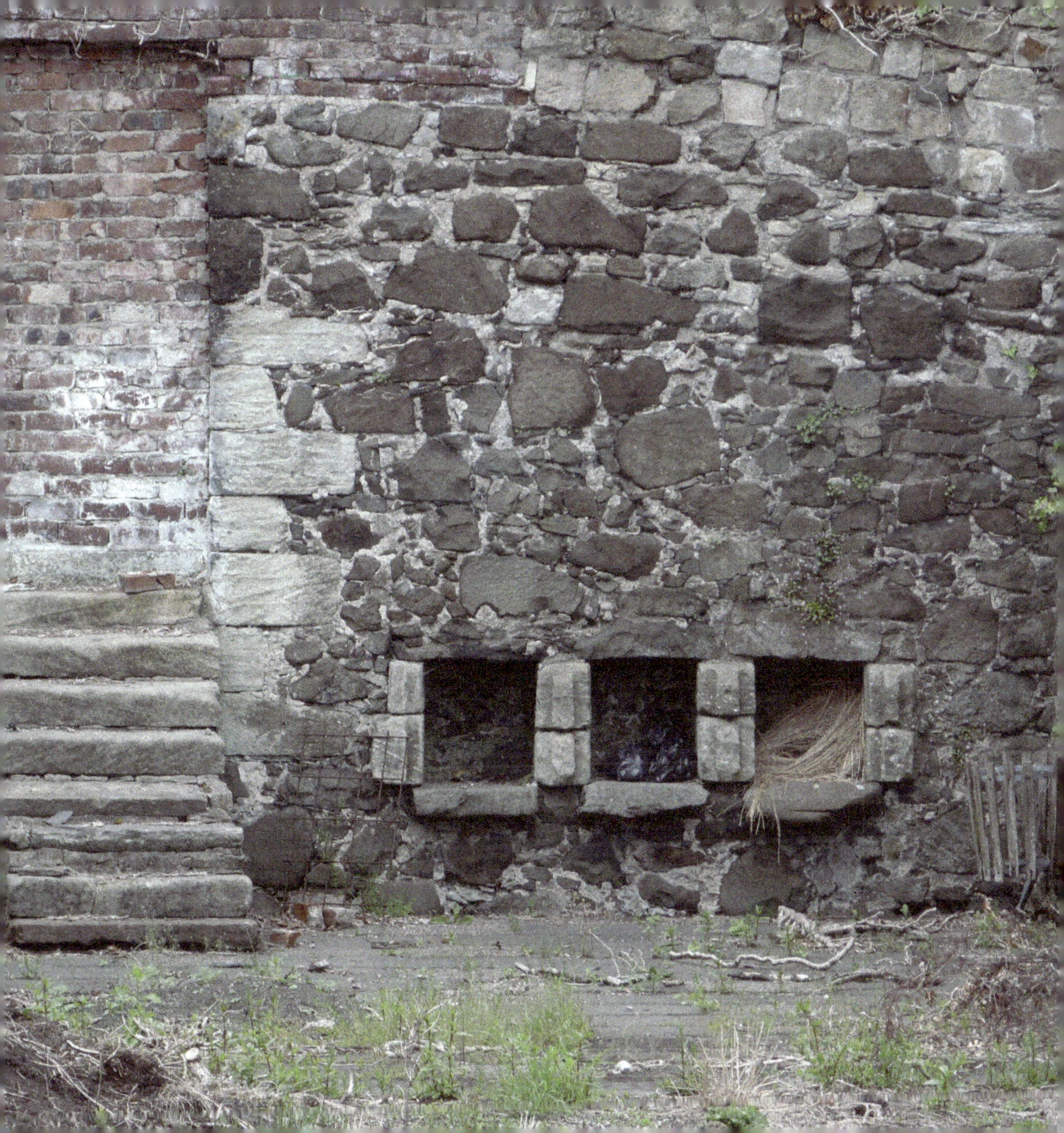

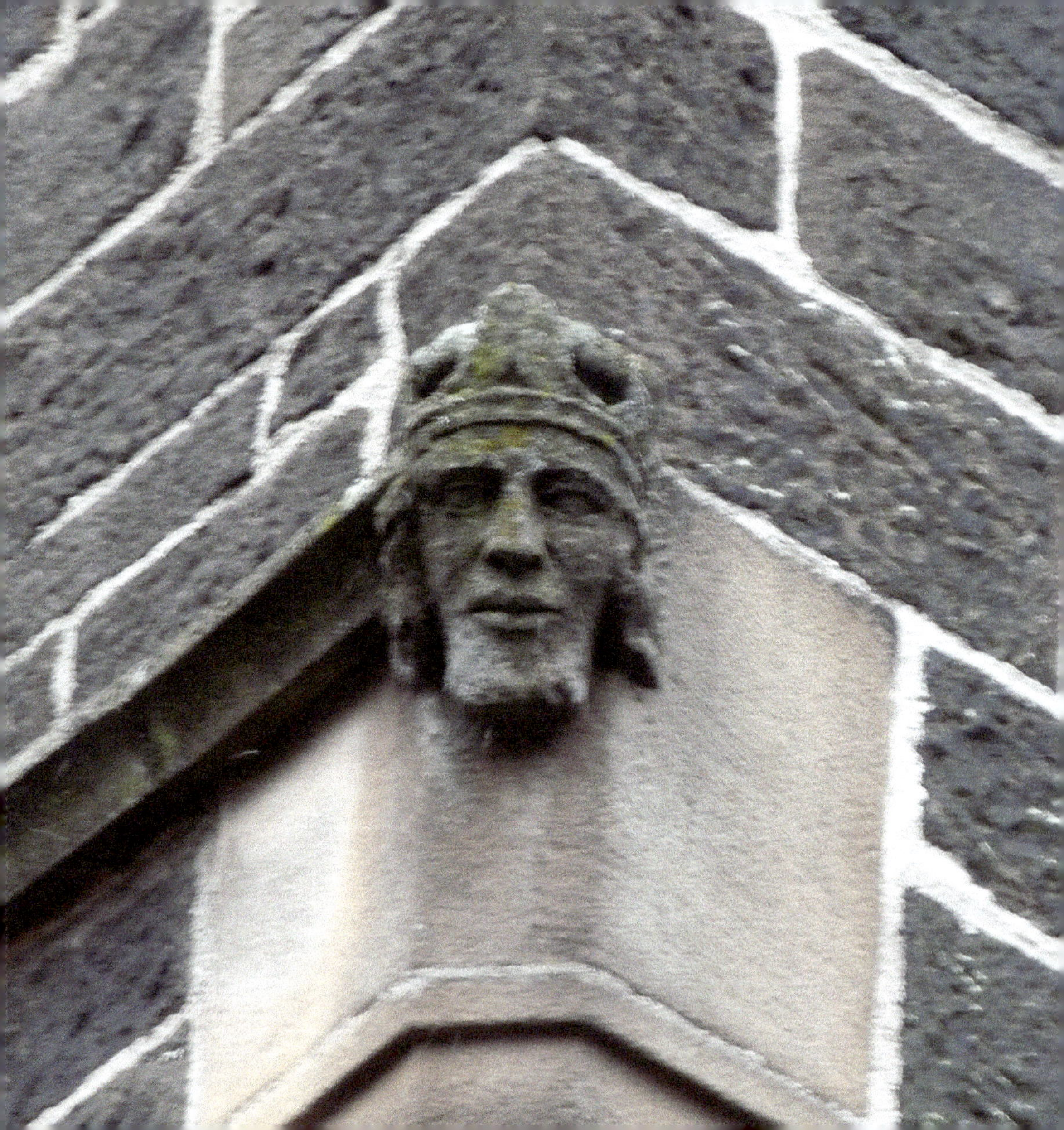

David I
The King that Made Scotland?

Now, lots of monarchs left their mark on Stirling. Alexander I died here; Mary, Queen of Scots was born here; and Bruce's reputation was made here. But David I made Stirling and helped transform Scotland into a modern European state by introducing English and European reforms, so that historians sometimes talk of a Davidian Revolution. So what did David I do for Stirling? Well, he established the Burgh in around 1124, then he established the High School and Cambuskenneth Abbey, and I happen to think he probably built the first bridge that was later destroyed during the Battle of Stirling Bridge. Oh, and he also had Scotland's only Royal Saint, St Margaret, for a mum!

The reason I argue for David building the bridge is that, as we heard, during his father's time there was no bridge and Stirling was not yet part of Scotland. David's father, Malcolm III (the one from Macbeth), was a very bloody and successful king and far from the meek mild lamb of the play—he seems to be the only Scottish king to have killed both of his predecessors! Anyway, you wouldn't build a bridge until you had secured Stirling, as the Forth was your biggest ally against invaders. It's likely that David's elder brother Edgar built the Castle and that his other older brother, Alexander I, expanded it. Having two elder brothers, no one really expected David to inherit the crown. He was given a semi-independent region: the northern rump of the kingdom of Northumberland, which covered most of Glasgow, Lothian, the Borders, and Dumfries and Galloway. His father and brothers ruled the core of Scotland between the Forth and Moray Firth; this area was called Alba. When his brothers died, he inherited their kingdom too, and the border was pushed far to the south, making it safe to build a bridge over the Forth!

NS 79424 93544

Secrets of The Municipal Building 1
The Viking and the Wolf

As you've heard, Stirling is Scotland's smallest city, and is very proud of the rich and wonderful history all bursting out from such a tiny wee place. And most if it is even true. This history is celebrated through the Council's Municipal Buildings; a wonderful, ambitious Edwardian evocation of Empire and history. However, unfortunately only half of it was built due to a lack of funds.

The building bristles with images of Bruce, Wallace, Mary, Queen of Scots and much, much more. I used to work there and spent lunches and coffee breaks exploring dusty nooks and crannies, but without a camera. I went back and asked the building's current occupiers, the very friendly CodeBase, to let me wander around... and they did.

The picture is of the finials of the main staircase, and features two wonderful oak carvings: a crouching Viking holding a now-lost sword (probably removed for Health and Safety reasons!) and a snarling ferocious wolf. What a welcome for visitors! So what is going on? Well, legend has it that around 900 AD Stirling was threatened by a horde of raiding Vikings. The guard at the southern gate fell asleep and the Vikings, no doubt after slitting the guard's throat, were about to start a rampage when they disturbed a wolf in some nearby rocks. The wolf's howls roused the town, and the Vikings were chased away. To this day, the rocks where the wolf apparently lay are known as Wolf Craig, and the wolf is the symbol of our proud burgh. You can even see a wolf on the side of the building. But is the story true? Hmm... er, oh dear, probably not precisely. But—and it's a big but—the Vikings did raid this area, and the fort on the Abbey Craig was contemporary... so perhaps the legend garbles Stirling for Abbey Craig?

Unfortunately the stair case is not open to the public, but you can view lots from the outside!

NS 79495 93400

NO ENTRY

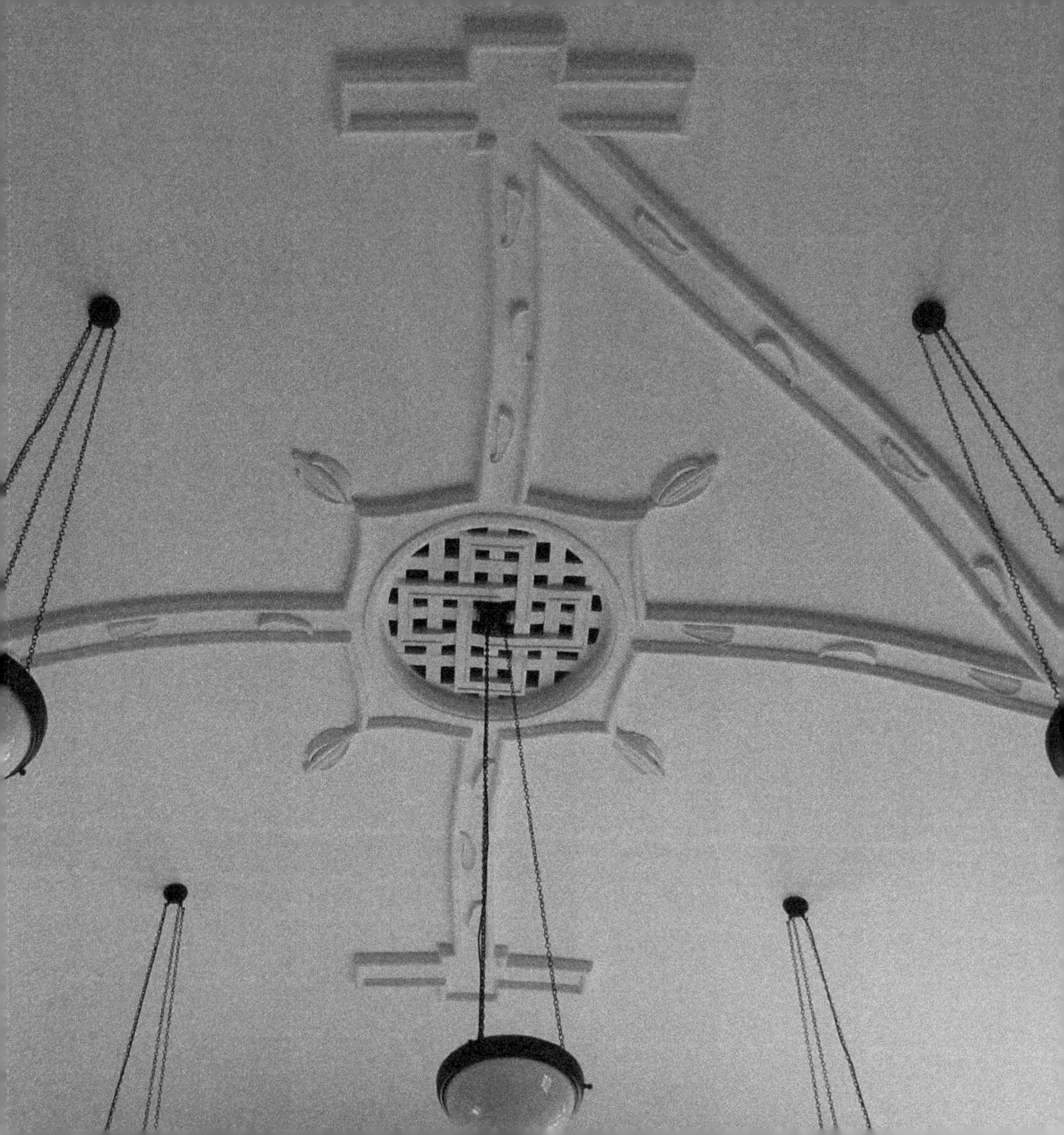

Secrets of The Municipal Building 2

The Biggest 4 in Scotland... and It's Backwards!

One of the rooms in the Municipal Building celebrates what might be the oldest continuously running civic organisation in Scotland, indeed the third oldest institution in Scotland, after the Church and the Crown. Stirling's Merchant's Guild, or 'the Guildry' as it is known, claims to have been founded during Alexander I's reign in 1119. Now this is a bit tricky, as technically you can't have a guildry without a Burgh, and the Burgh wasn't founded until at least 1124 by Alexander's younger brother, David. The Guildry ensured production standards amongst the various trades: Hammermen (metal workers), Skinners (leather makers), Bakers, Weavers, Tailors, Fleshers (butchers) and Shoemakers. This also allowed the King to raise taxes: he created burghs, and Merchant Guilds paid for the right to operate in a Burgh which created a monopoly for them.

The backwards 4 is their symbol, and represents honesty and fair dealing between merchants. The symbol itself is much older, and may have its origin in Baltic trade. It appears on a variety of objects and media: church windows, furniture, grave stones, and even pies! The pies were given out at meetings for Guild members to gift to their wives, to demonstrate that they had attended a Guild meeting. The oldest example of the symbol is on a grave stone dating to 1511.

The most famous member of the Guildry was John Cowane, the head (or Dean) of the Guildry as well as Stirling's MP. He left the equivalent of £3 million to Stirling to create a charity for members of the Guildry who fell on hard times. The charity is still running today and manages the wonderful Cowane's Hospital, Scotland's best preserved alms house. John's statue sits above its door, and he's known as Auld Staneybreeks (remember his bees?). Legend has it he dances a jig at the stroke of midnight every Hogmanay!

Unfortunately this room is not open to the public, but you can view a lot from the outside!

NS 79495 93400

Secrets of The Municipal Building 3
A Multiplicity of Wallace's Swords
(Try Saying That After Three Pints!)

Once upon a time, Municipal Buildings had a live-in official: the Town Officer, who had his own house at the very top of the building with spectacular views. If you know where to look, you can also his find his lovely wee Art Deco bell by the front door. (The Chief Librarian's family also lived in a private flat over the road... but that is for another book.) Anyway, the Town Officer had to wash his clothes, and these would be put on a washing line on a roof terrace to dry. The roof terrace is protected by a wee fence, and its supports are made from replicas of Wallace's Sword (and yes, the capitals are deliberate), and there are half a dozen of them. These are surely the most incongruous things ever associated with Wallace.

Anyway, as you will all know, Wallace's Sword is proudly displayed in the National Wallace Monument and people can pose with a replica, but—and don't tell anyone—this is a replica of a replica. 'What?' I hear you splutter. 'I climbed all those steps to look not at Wallace's Sword, prized from his fingers over 700 years ago by the treacherous Earl of Menteith, but a [expletive deleted] replica? What's going on?' Pause... cool the jets, keep the heid; it's alright, it's not a con. The Wallace Sword is not really a well-preserved 13th century weapon—it's made of at least three different swords, and has a new handle. It is the sword presented to James IVth as Wallace's Sword in around 1500. I think that the original Wallace Sword looked a bit scabby after 200 years rusting away, so it was 'tidied up' a bit—a big sword for Scotland's greatest hero, who had become an even bigger legend. But perhaps protecting washing is just a wee bit beneath his dignity!

Unfortunately the roof terrace is not open to the public, but you can view them from the outside in the rear car park.

NS 79495 93400

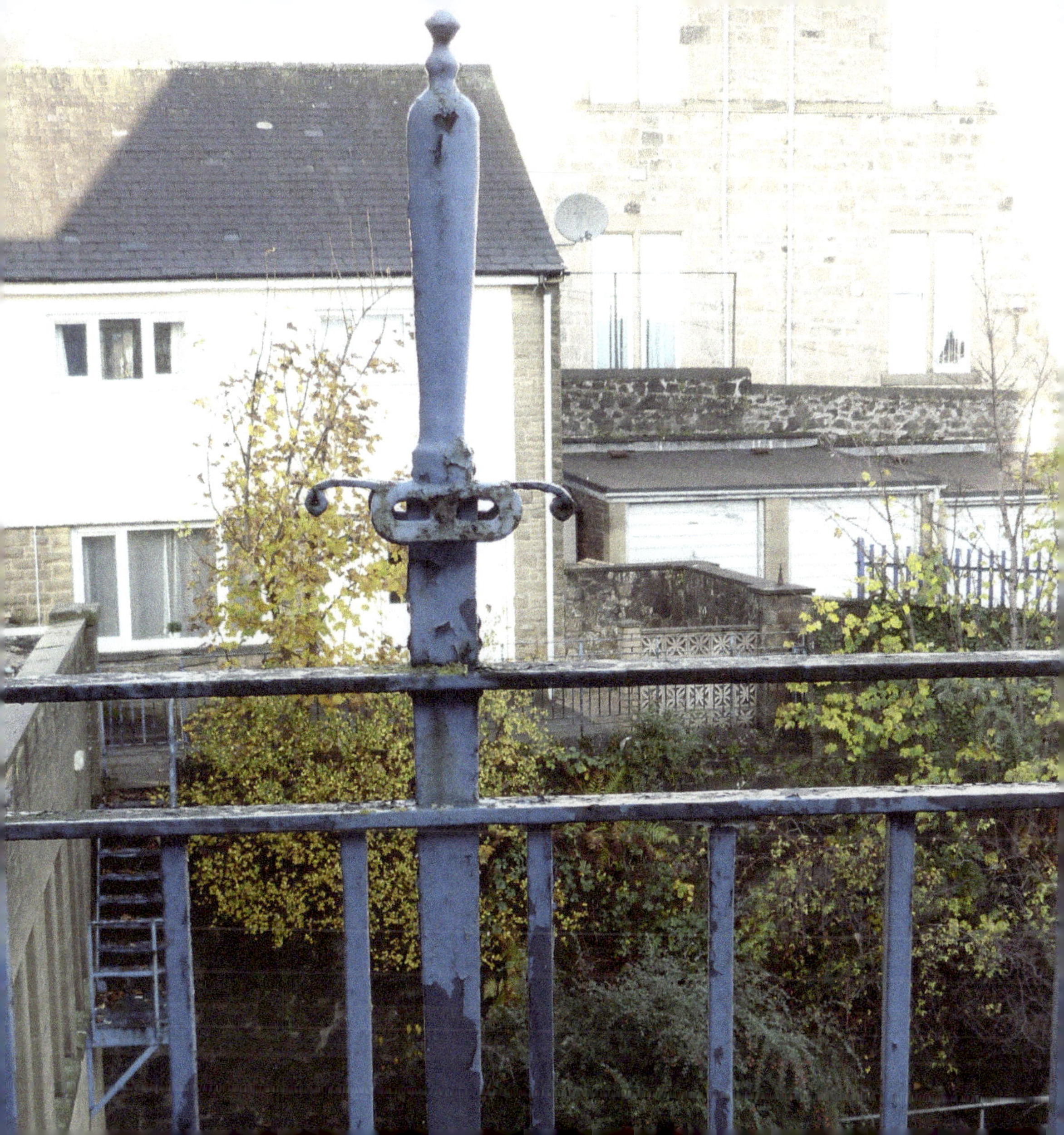

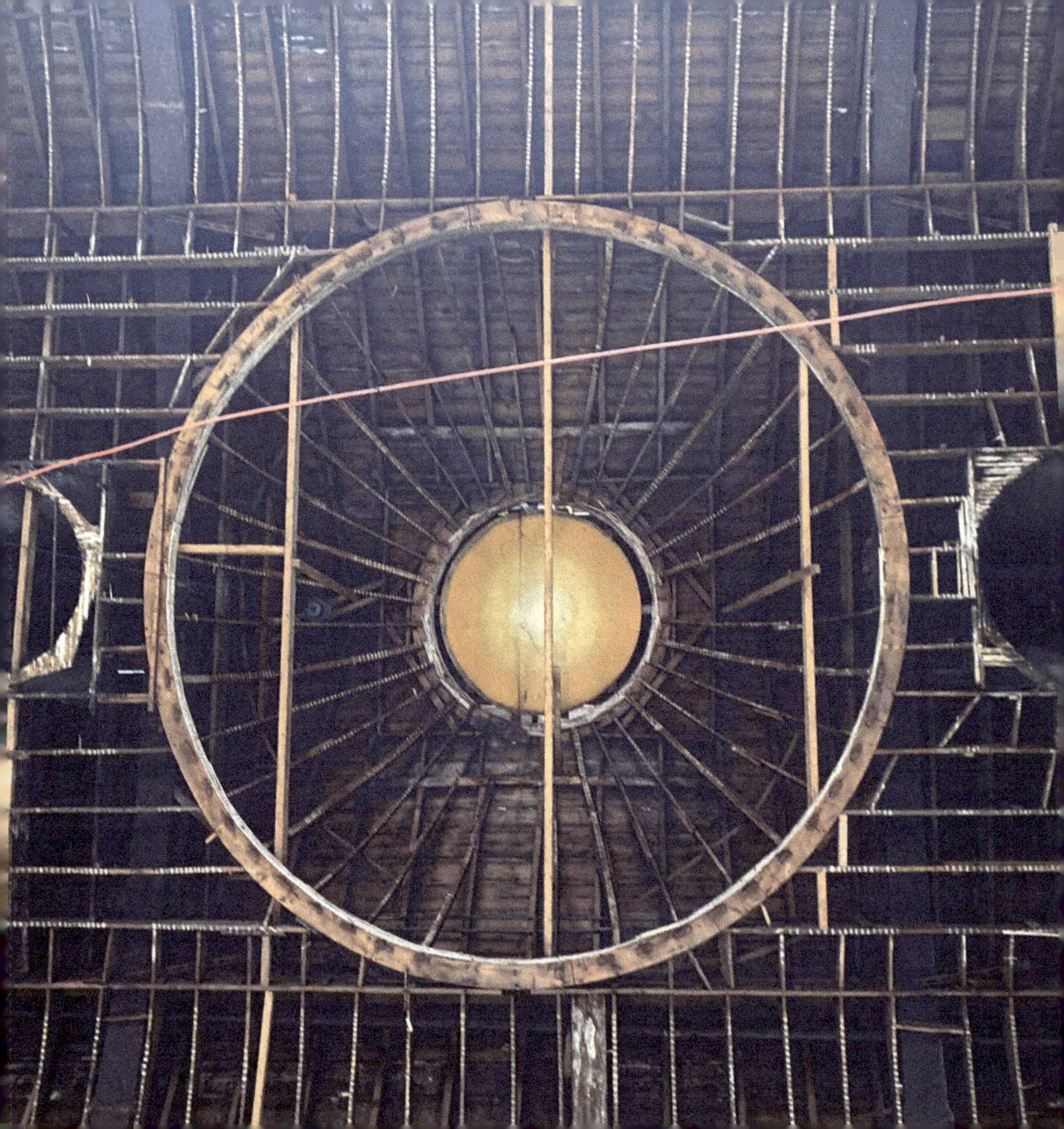

Skeletons and Axes
A Lost Theatre

When it's wet and cold (so, a typical Scottish summer?), Stirling has two key indoor shopping experiences. The biggest is The Thistles, and I'll talk about that below, but the classiest is the Victorian Arcade: one of only a handful in Scotland. It was designed by John McLean and paid for by William Crawford (he and his family have a magnificent grave in the Old Town Cemetery). This amazing structure originally held two hotels, six flats and 39 shops, and cost £30,000 to construct in 1879. But this lovely dog-legged short cut to and from the train station has a dangerous secret at its heart. The key attraction of the Arcade was the Alhambra Theatre, which was opened in 1882 and has seen all of its magnificent, richly decorated roof stripped away over the years, leaving an enormous abandoned leaky skeletal framework. The owner, Mr Kevin Moore, is trying to save this majestic edifice and find a new use. Good luck to him.

We know that Sir Harry Lauder performed here, but too little research has been done yet for us to know who else might have done. Roughly 500 people a night were entertained here, 50 years before it was converted to a cinema in 1931. The cinema didn't last long, and was closed in 1939. The building then became a series of shops and offices, and sometime over that period the ornate ceiling was stripped away. For years, the space was neglected and unloved, with a series of persistent leaks. It is now being saved and hopefully will open to customers again. But how do you use such a space? At the moment it is home to Game of Throwing, Stirling's only axe throwing venue... great fun!

NS 79638 93445

Mr Burns Gets into Trouble

No, not that one; rather darling Scotia's National Bard—Rabbie himself—who was in Stirling in August 1787 and feasted in the Golden Lion Hotel, which is why Stirling has an annual Burns Supper on the 29th August to celebrate his visit here. While he had fun, he was a bit disappointed in Stirling; this was the ancient core of our kingdom, from where we defied Edwards I and II. Eighteenth century Stirling was smelly (open sewers) and a bit corrupt. Infamously, the Black Bond of 1771 had comprised an agreement between city officials to divvy up positions and income between themselves. This was so bad that in 1773, the Council elections were declared void by the courts, 'having been brought about by undue influence and corrupted practices,' and the Council was abolished until 1781. Just a few years earlier, the incredible Renaissance carved heads in James V's magnificent palace had fallen off, and the building was stripped to be converted to a barracks.

As Burns angrily put it on a window in the Golden Lion, the aforementioned hotel in Stirling:

Here Stewarts once in triumph reign'd,
And laws for Scotland's weal ordain'd;
But now unroof'd their Palace stands,
Their sceptre's fall'n to other hands;
Fallen indeed, and to the earth,
Whence grovelling reptiles take their birth.
The injur'd STEWART-line are gone,
A Race outlandish fill their throne;
An idiot race, to honor lost;
Who know them best despise them most.

He soon regretted his defiance and, despite smashing the glass, the poem's seditious tone haunted his later life—he revealed that he had been '...questioned like a child... and blamed and schooled for my... Stirling inscription'. A replica of the inscription has been made for the hotel bar.

NS 79647 93376

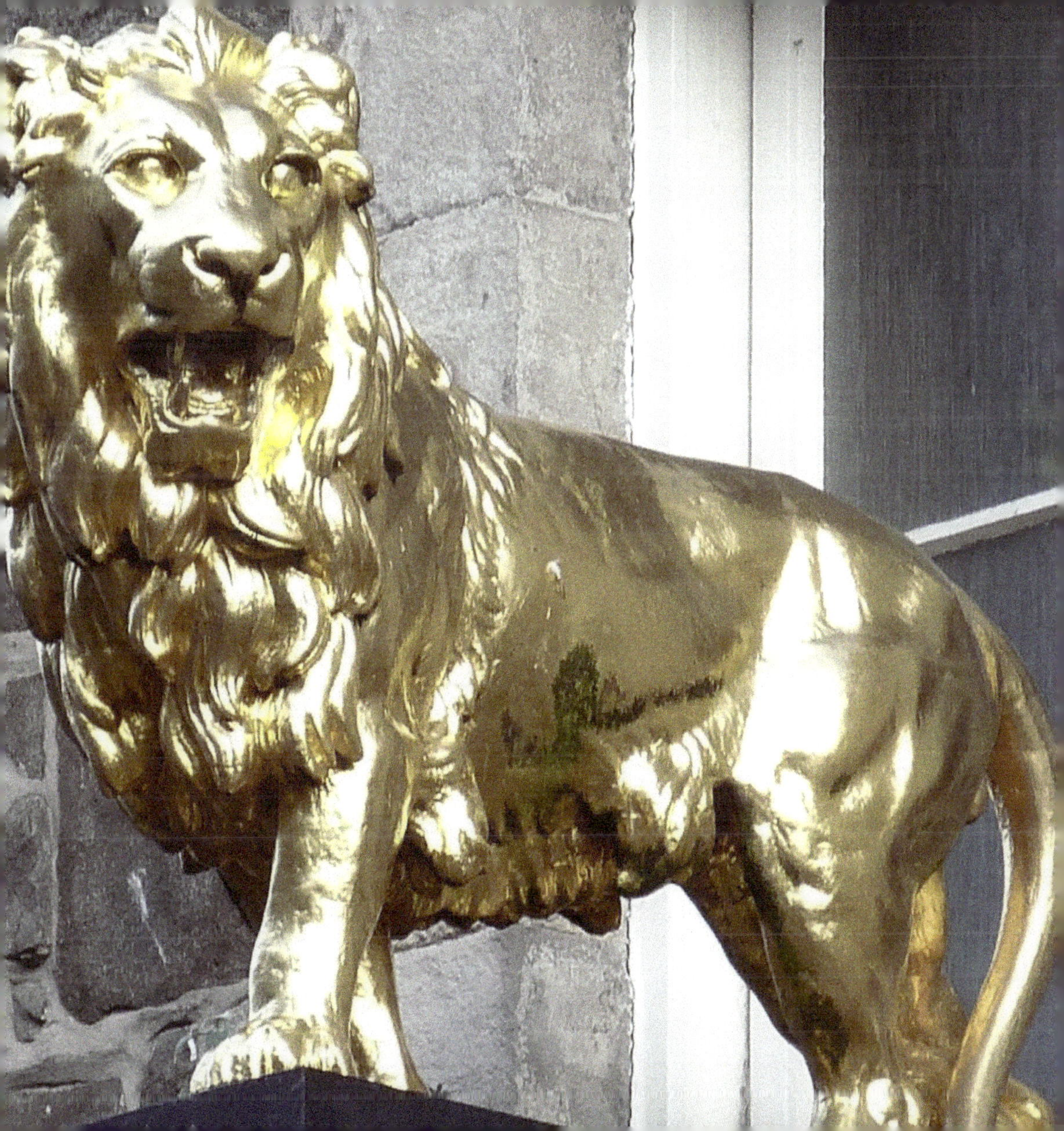

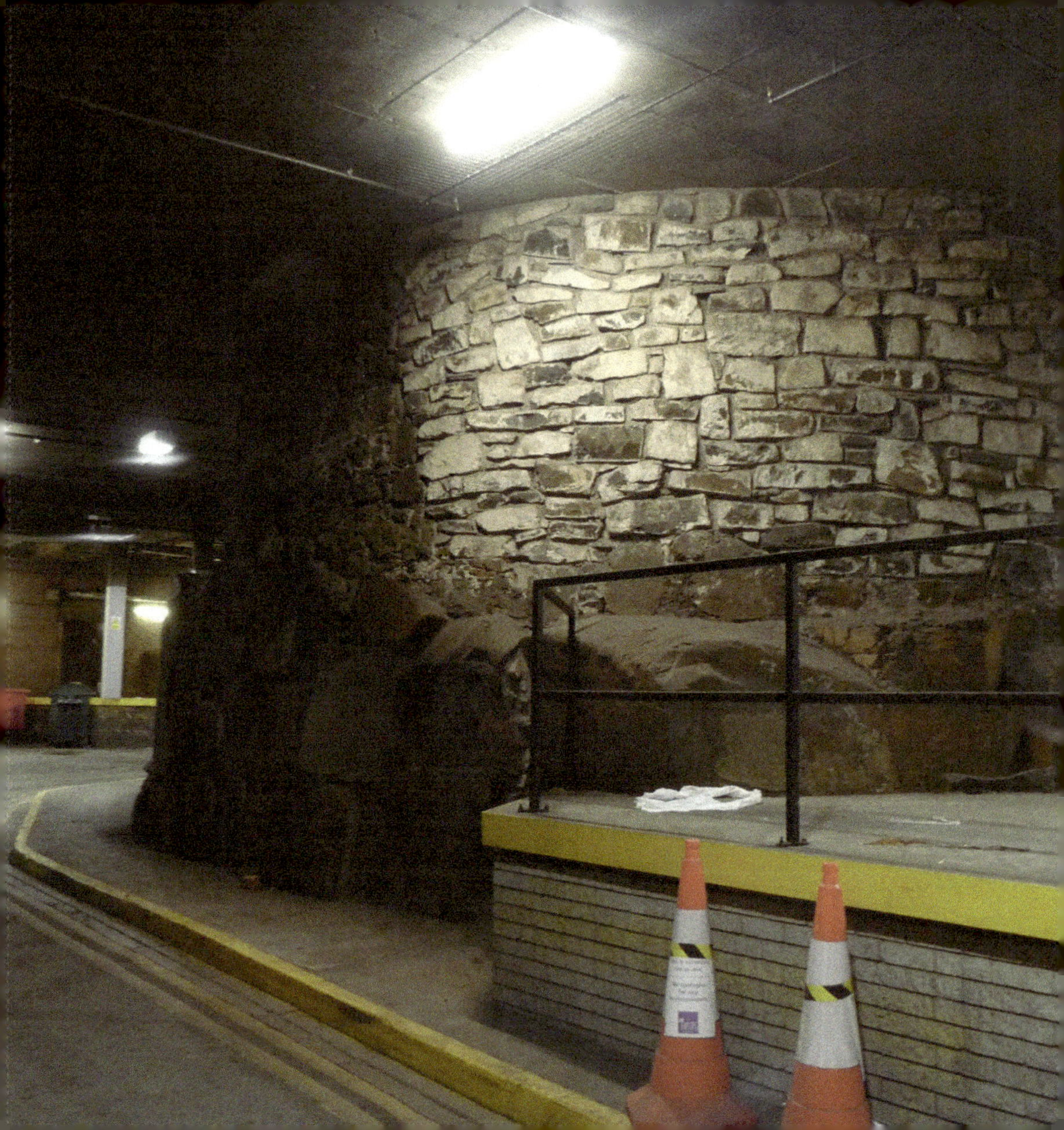

Stirling's Buried Street

You've heard how Stirling has Scotland's best preserved city walls. The eastern section ran behind Port Street (port is Scots for gate), and was demolished in Stirling's late 18th and 19th century expansion. The road outside the wall was known as Dirt Raw, and the gate that ran through the wall, the Dirt Raw Port—though it was really only a hole that got blocked up. The gate was protected by a round tower, which contained a cannon trained on the gate. The last time the tower was used in anger was in January 1746, when Stirling was under siege from Bonnie Prince Charlie's Jacobites. As Stirling became more refined, Dirt Raw was renamed Orchard Place to boost house prices, and at one point held a roller-skating rink.

Both the round tower and Orchard Place were sealed under the Thistles Shopping Centre when it was built in the 1970s. Today, the upper portions can be visited as a tourist attraction in the Thistles called The Thieves' Pot—a pit dungeon with a very small toilet in the corner. You can see the lower portions if you drive under the Thistles to its car park. However, I had always wanted to see more, so one day went for a look. I spoke to someone I thought was in charge, and they said okay. Within ten minutes, I noticed two Security Guards performing a pincer movement on me. Aha! Whoever I had spoken to was clearly not in charge! The two very polite but firm chaps escorted me outside. However, I went back and made a formal appointment, and eventually walked to the tower and the site of Dirt Raw Port and along buried and silent Orchard Place as shoppers scurried above my head. There I spotted a number of previously unrecorded musket ball impacts... wow!

There is no access to the exterior.

NS 79731 93278

20
Warring Bedfellows

What connects Edward I, Robert the Bruce, William Wallace, a Regent of Scotland, and a pretender to the English throne? Why... Stirling's former Dominican Priory, which sat opposite what would become the train station and is now flats. It was founded in 1233 and destroyed in the Reformation by what must been Scotland's angriest mob, who marched from Perth to Stirling intent on sacking Catholic places of worship.

The Dominicans came to Stirling as part of an international deal that saw Queen Margaret, the wife of Malcolm III and the mother of David I, get made a saint. This would've been one of the more impressive and important places in Stirling, and definitely fit for a king, which is why both Edward and Robert stayed here—though not together. It was from the Priory that Friars walked to Stirling Bridge on the 11th September 1297 to try to negotiate peace. They spoke with Wallace and De Moray, who refused, and then Wallace met his destiny and achieved an incredible victory.

The Regent was Murdoch, Duke of Albany; he was James I's cousin, and his father Robert had captured James' elder brother David and starved him to death! (Gosh, I bet that made Christmas awkward.) While fleeing, James ended up getting captured by the English. Murdoch was slow in paying the ransom, and so he was beheaded for treason and buried in the cemetery. Of course, there was then an even bloodier reprisal, and James ended up dying of stab wounds, in a drain, under a tennis court in Perth. 'But what about the pretender to the English throne?' I hear you cry. Ah, that was the Mammet King; someone who claimed to be Richard II. No one believed him, and when he died he was buried here!

NS 79726 93565

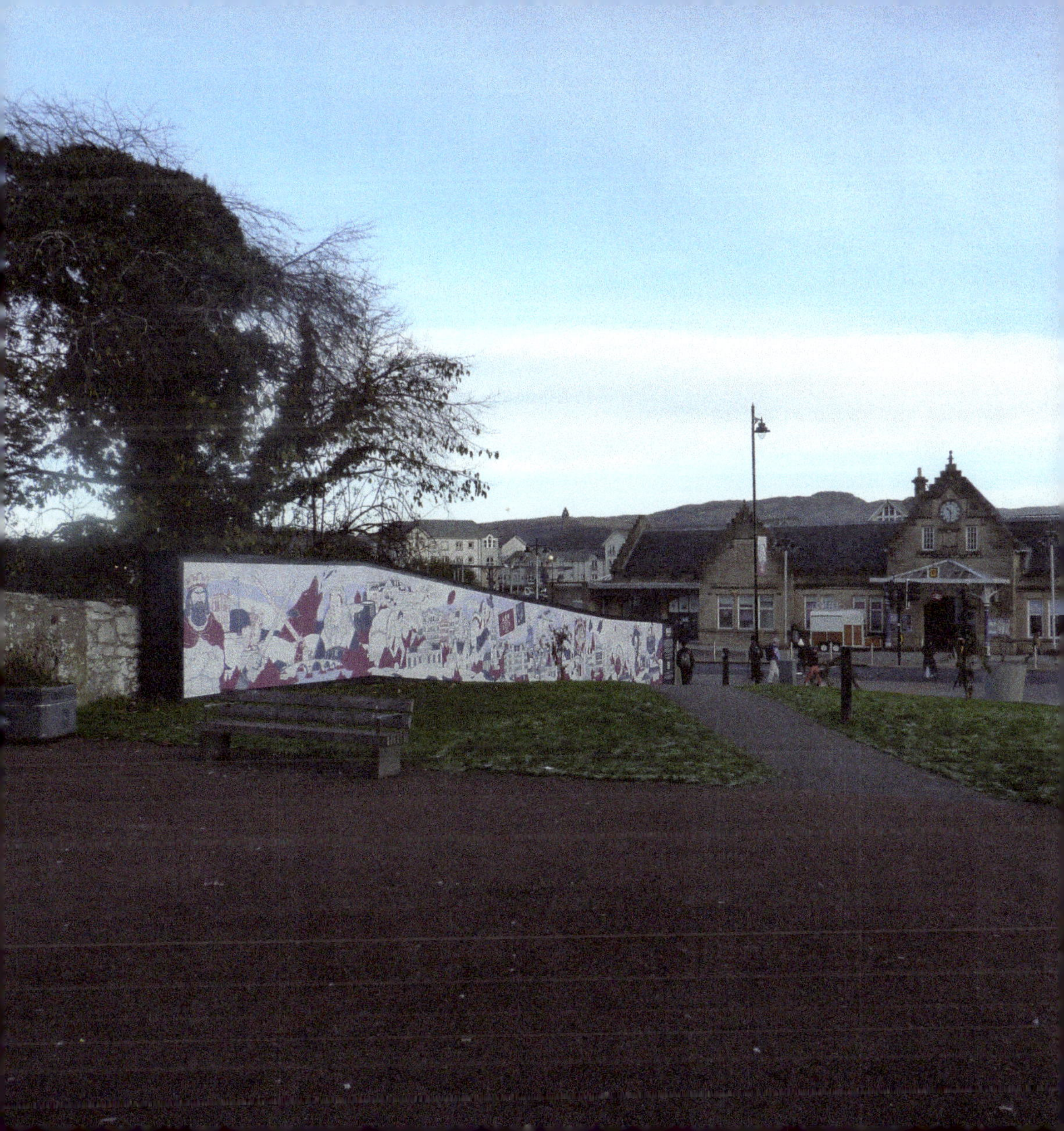

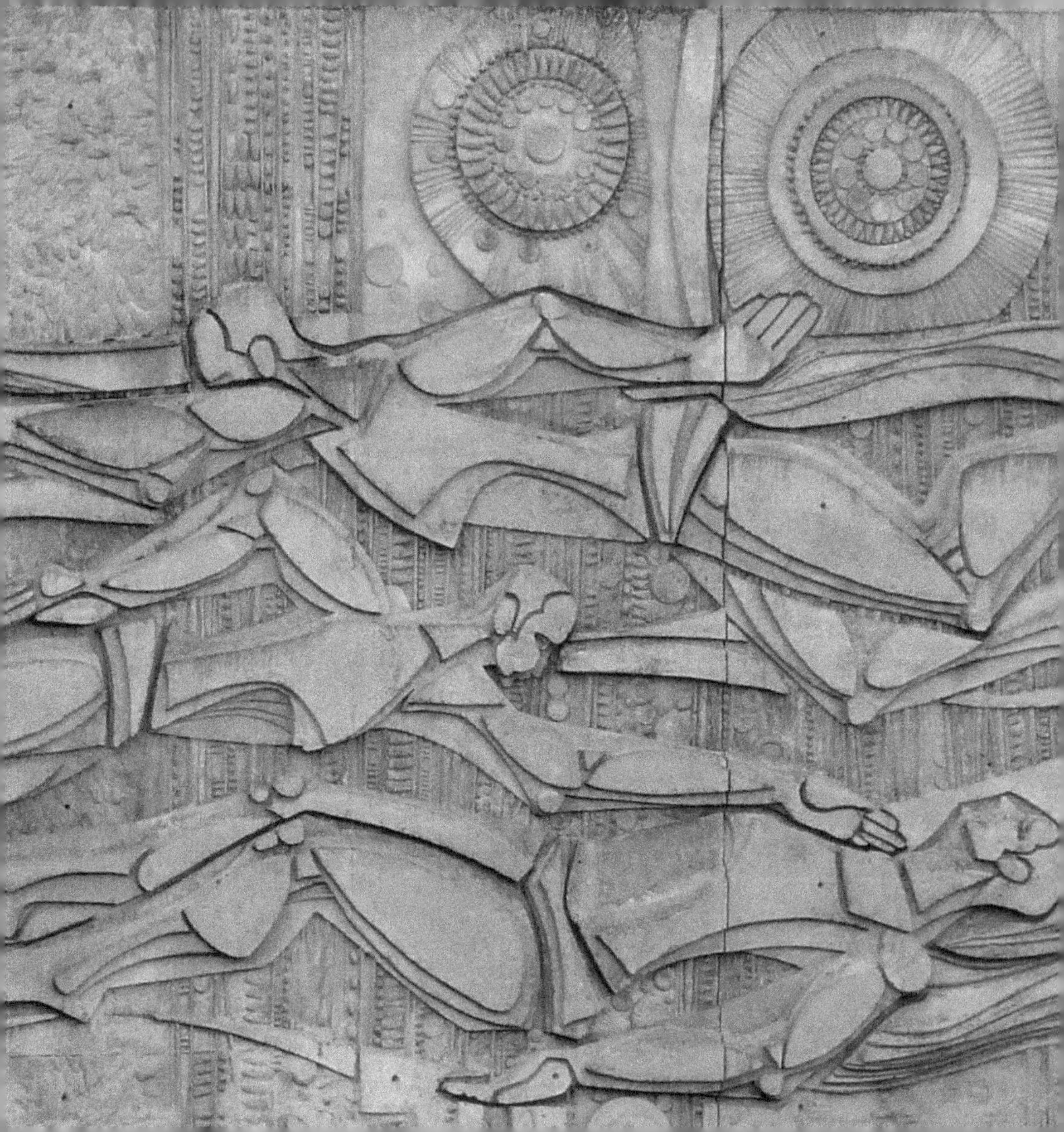

The Stank at The Provost's Pool

No, this is not a story of local government corruption, but the discovery of a medieval defensive ditch known as The Stank (because it was full of smelly water). This ditch was under Stirling's 1970s swimming baths, known initially as the Provost's Pool and then Rainbow Slides, after water slides had been added. The wall of the pool had an amazing sculpture of people swimming by local artist Charles Anderson (pictured), all very 1970s.

Stirling's wall protected the south, as to the north was boggy ground but also Stirling Bridge, the best preserved medieval bridge in Scotland. The ground was made even more defensive by a series of inter-cutting drainage ditches that took sewage from the city into the Forth (yuck!). During Cromwell's invasion, this system needed to be strengthened. But rather than pay for it to be done, the then-Provost offered to buy anyone who helped a drink—it's not recorded if this offer was accepted. Over time, the ditch was forgotten, filled in and built on and only rediscovered when the site was to be redeveloped. I recommended that an archaeological evaluation be done, and this uncovered a massive, 6m wide, 2m deep ditch that had survived a pool being built on top of it! The ditch was finally destroyed when a hotel was constructed (it is after all very hard to preserve a smelly hole in the ground), but of course a full record of the ditch was made. But what of Charles Anderson's sculpture? Surely that wasn't demolished? No, it was preserved by the builders, Ogilvie Group, who reinstalled it at their headquarters (NS 80207 89593).

NS 79658 93858

Sir William Wallace's Real HQ
and The Road to Victory?

Tens of thousands of tourists each year climb the 300 million year old rugged volcanic fist of the Abbey Craig to look at The National Wallace Monument, Britain's largest memorial to an individual. They do the tour and buy a present, or get an excellent scone in Legends Café, and think about the Scots who stood here and watched the approach of the English army and planned. The Victorians thought that the ancient hillfort here (the low grassy bank to the rear of the monument is far older, and was perhaps built to deter raiding Vikings) was Wallace's headquarters, but we don't think that any more—if for no other reason than getting down would be hard. I have wondered about Causewayhead Park at the bottom of what was once sea cliffs, but I think the most likely spot is a location now partially in the grounds of Stirling University.

This location is called Spittal Hill, which seems to be connected to the site of a former medieval hospital (a monastic foundation, and not an A&E!). In the 19th century, workmen apparently disturbed a cemetery, and there are medieval records from the 13th century of a hospital dedicated to St James which was destroyed during the Reformation. Some have even argued that the site belonged to the Templars, though there is no evidence for that. It strikes me that this low hill associated with a religious location is far more likely a candidate for the Scots than the higher Abbey Craig. However, even if that does not convince you, a section of the original medieval road that led to the Bridge, used by Wallace and the Scots as they marched to destiny, lies just to the east again in the University's grounds, and this is the only place in Stirling where you can walk exactly where Wallace and his heroes marched (NS 80693 95860).

NS 80642 96002

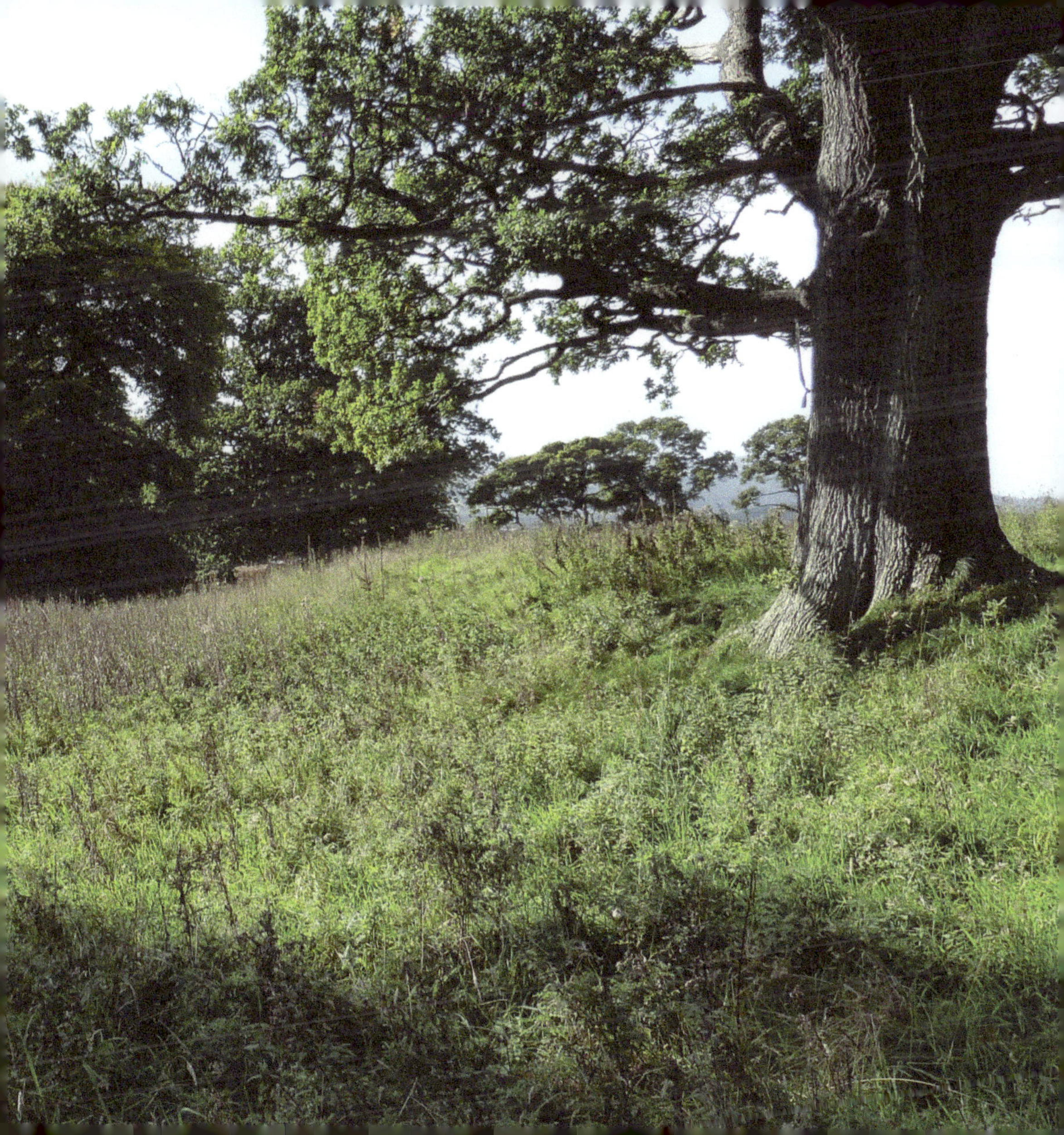

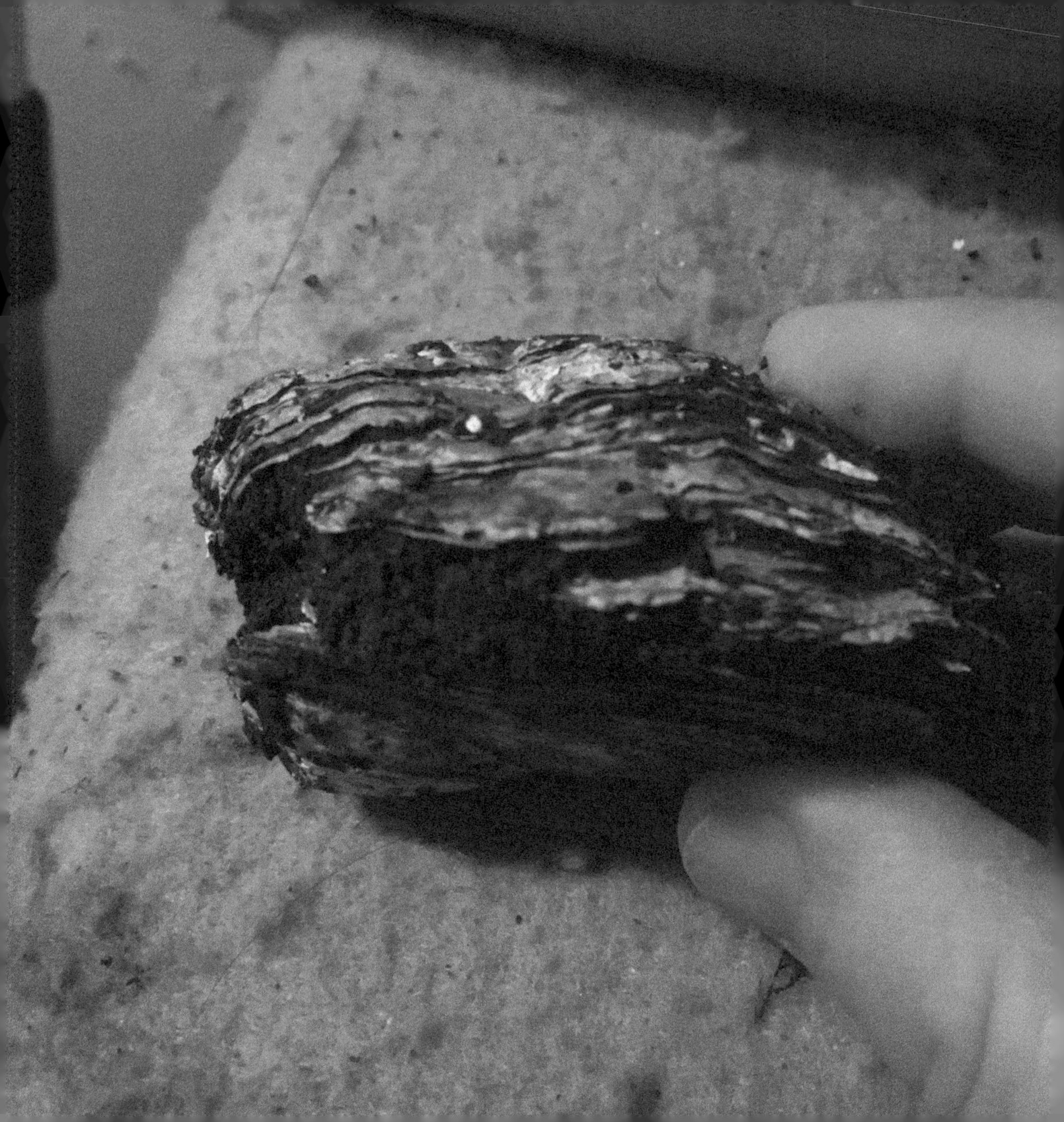

Bridge of Allan-on-Sea
and a 6,000 Year Old Oyster

Global warming is an existential threat to all of us. At a local level, flood maps for 2050 show large chunks of residential areas like Riverside and Raploch under water—again. I say this because most of the Forth Valley was under water 10,000 years ago. After the last ice age, whales swam over Throsk and Fallin, and Cambusbarron would have been a coastal town with a sandy beach.

While this is an established fact, it's very hard to imagine, and it's easier if you can see the physical remains of these things. At the confluence of the Allan Water and The Forth, between Bridge of Allan and Cornton, there's an eroding line of marine oyster shells which was reported to me by a member of the public. I got very excited; perhaps it was a shell midden from our ancient ancestors? But when I went for a look, it was clear that it wasn't just a rubbish dump: the line was too thin, it was all oysters, and some were still closed. In fact, this turned out to be the remains of an oyster reef from when the area was under the sea... but when was that, exactly? To figure this out, I needed to get a shell and get it dated: a trickier prospect than it sounds. This portion of the river is tidal and the mud is very, very slippy. My waders filled up with water and I fell in twice... groan! But I dug a shell out and had it radiocarbon dated, which indicated that it died between 4037–3663 BC, around 6,000 years ago. This was when the first farmers were arriving in Scotland, and it's older than the Egyptian Pyramids. It's simply awesome what lies below our feet if you stop to look! But if we're not more careful with our carbon emissions we may lose it all.

The oyster bed is best viewed from the eastern bank of the Allan Water, and I really don't recommend getting into the water.

NS 78555 96412

Robert Louis Stevenson
Bridge of Allan and Treasure Island

Robert Louis Stevenson—the sickly boy from the family of engineers, whose imagination created such classics as *Dr Jekyll and Mr Hyde* (surely the inspiration for the Hulk?), *Treasure Island* and, my favourite, *Kidnapped*—is Scotland's most translated author. Yet he died in Samoa at only 44.

Our very own Bridge of Allan was the family's summer home for nearly two decades, and they all got to know the area very well. The town seems to have inspired much from his novels. Dr Paterson (who we will hear of again) treated the young Lou (as he was known in the family), and the local pharmacist Gilbert Farie, who scared wee Lou, seems to have been the source of Dr Jekyll and respectively Mr Hyde. An old mine may have become Ben Gunn's cave (the marooned pirate who craved cheese), and an island next to the confluence of the Allan Water and The Forth (next to our lost oyster bed) may have been the island from *Treasure Island* and also appears in *Kidnapped*. Lou and his little cousin Charlie used to wander down and play on the island, and apparently even carved their initials on tree trunks next to it.

Now, I have walked past and waded to this spot several times and even wandered on the island—and whenever I go, Lou's self penned epigraph comes back to me:

Under the wide and starry sky,
Dig the grave and let me lie
Glad did I live an gladly die,
And I laid me down with a will

This be the verse you grave for me,
Here he lies where he longed to be;
Home is the sailor home from the sea,
And the hunter home from the hill.

NS 78838 96319

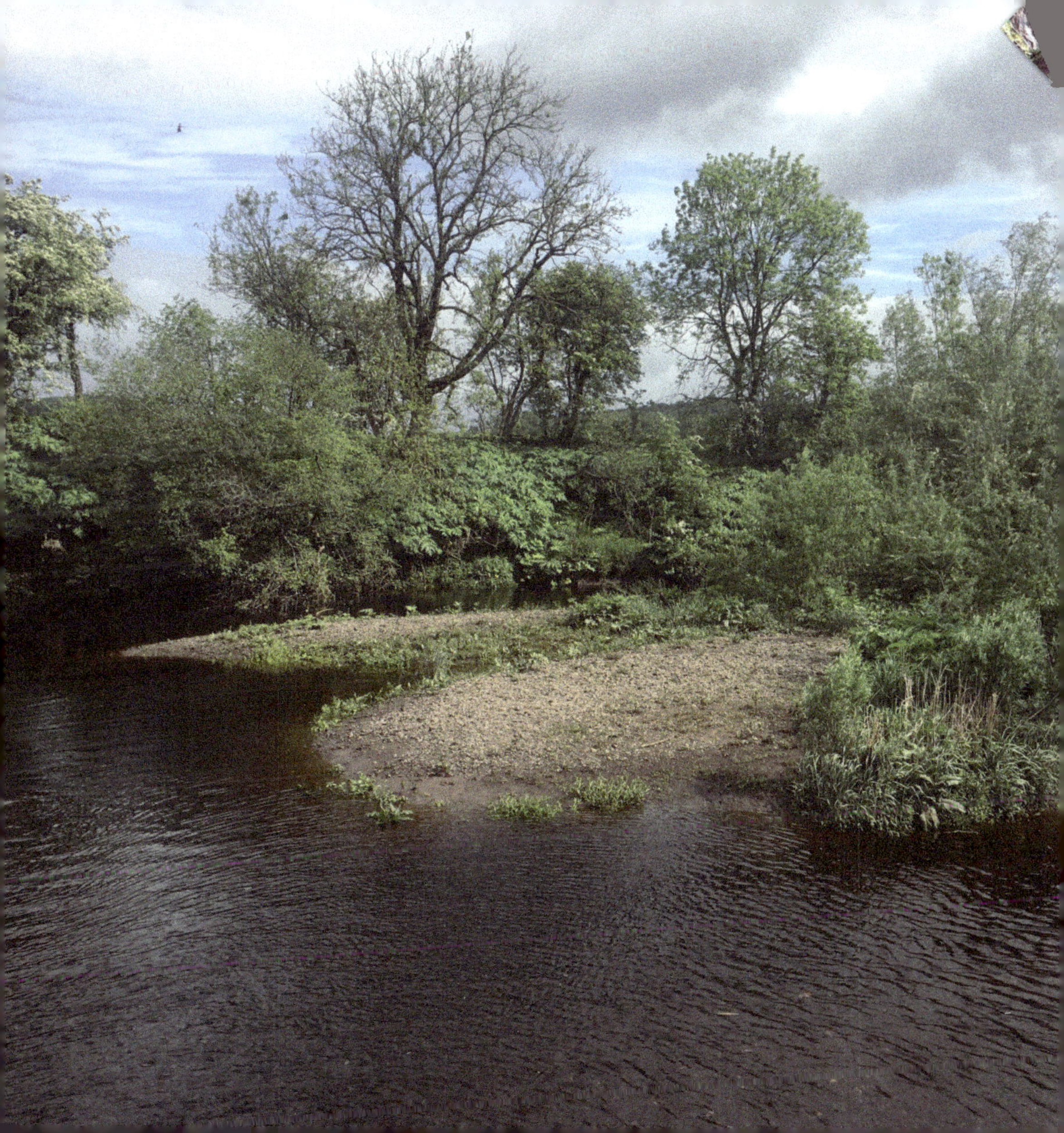

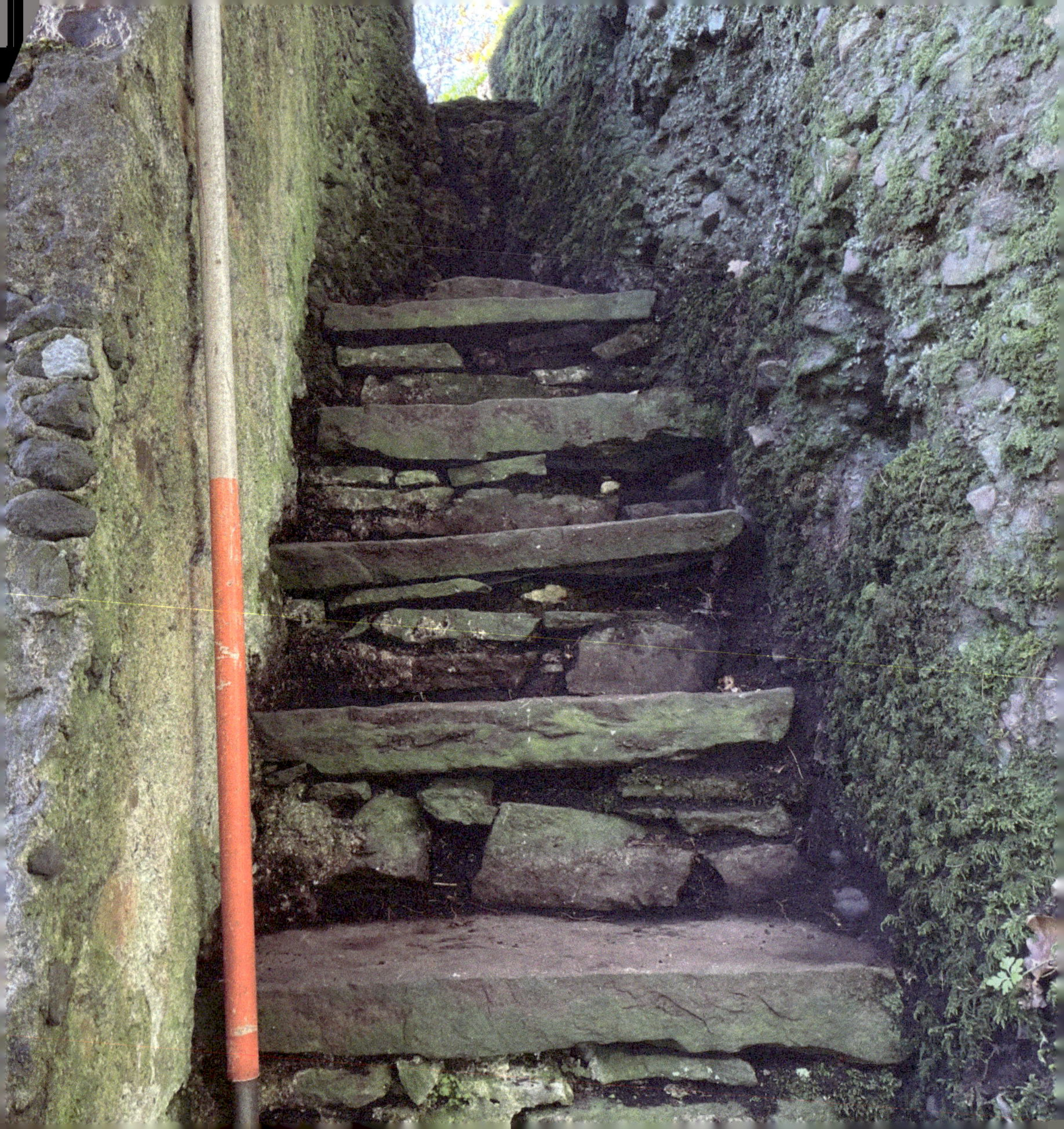

The Hermit of Bridge of Allan
and Scotland's Most Expensive Joke!

No, this is not a story about a retired, grumpy former academic from Stirling University but rather the 18th century whim of a very, very rich man... not quite a Rockefeller, but certainly the equivalent of a modern multi-millionaire. The Airthrey Estate, which now houses Stirling University, was once owned by the Haldane family, who made their money in the East India Company. Robert Haldane inherited the estate when he was four years old in 1768. After a brief career in the Navy and a tour of Europe, he returned to redesign the landscape around the estate, which he enclosed in a wall. On the high cliffs to the north of the estate, he built a two-storey summer house and a hermitage; the latter an early example of a rustic folly. The building was small with a fireplace and viewing platform, with a staircase to a higher view—both of which are excellent. The walls were lined with a mixture of shells and little stones, and there were coloured windows. It was based on Oliver Goldsmith's famous poem by 'The Hermit', whose house was described thus:

Far in a wilderness obscure,
The lonely mansion lay;
A refuge to the neighbouring poor,
And strangers led astray.

Local tradition has it that a hermit was employed to live in it and pontificate on philosophical issues. However, he apparently became bored and left for a drinking session in Bridge of Allan. He was subsequently fired, and became both the first and last hermit—the family denied this, and it was apparently all an elaborate joke. The building was already neglected by 1800, and local children delighted in stealing the coloured glass. Today, the walls and roof are gone and it's a bit of scramble to reach it, but well worth gazing at those stairs and pondering the life of a hermit!

NS 80772 97002

Collected to Extinction
The Bridge of Allan Tea Plant

In 1879, Nellie Geddes from Bridge of Allan won the Bridge of Allan School Board's prize for the best wild flower collection from Lecropt Moss. But there was a problem: it contained a small, white-flowered shrub that no one could identify. Where had it come from? It couldn't be identified by either the School Board nor the Director of the Smith Institute, so a sample was sent to Kew and its Director, Sir Joseph Hooker: a man who had travelled on the ill-fated *Erebus* and encouraged Charles Darwin. Sir Joseph confirmed that it was *Ledum palustre*, which was found in America and known as Labrador tea because it was often used as a tea substitute by trappers. However, it became clear that this was not really Nellie's discovery, and had first been found by Dr Paterson, a local GP in 1860 (who had a clock dedicated to him[4] in Bridge of Allan, and who treated young Robert Louis Stevenson). There was tremendous excitement about an apparent native variety, and it became a must-have for plant collectors. By 1930 it had all been removed, and was apparently extinct. The plant equivalent of the Dodo: something rare and exotic destroyed by our greed?

However, how had such an exotic species got here? It seems likely that it was spread by birds rather than directly cultivated in the bog. However, were they from America or Scotland? There is still no answer to this mystery. However, if it was spread by birds then it makes sense that there might be other examples from the original source, wherever that was. And that has turned out to be the case—a recent article by Roy Sexton, Sarah Longrigg and John Snodin published in Volume 34 of the *Forth Naturalist and Historian* reveals that there are several other colonies in bogs across The Forth Valley. Of course, we are now concerned about invasive species, so perhaps we'll dig them all up again!

The location below is for Lecropt Moss, which is a lovely flat expanse with panoramic views.

NS 76489 97162

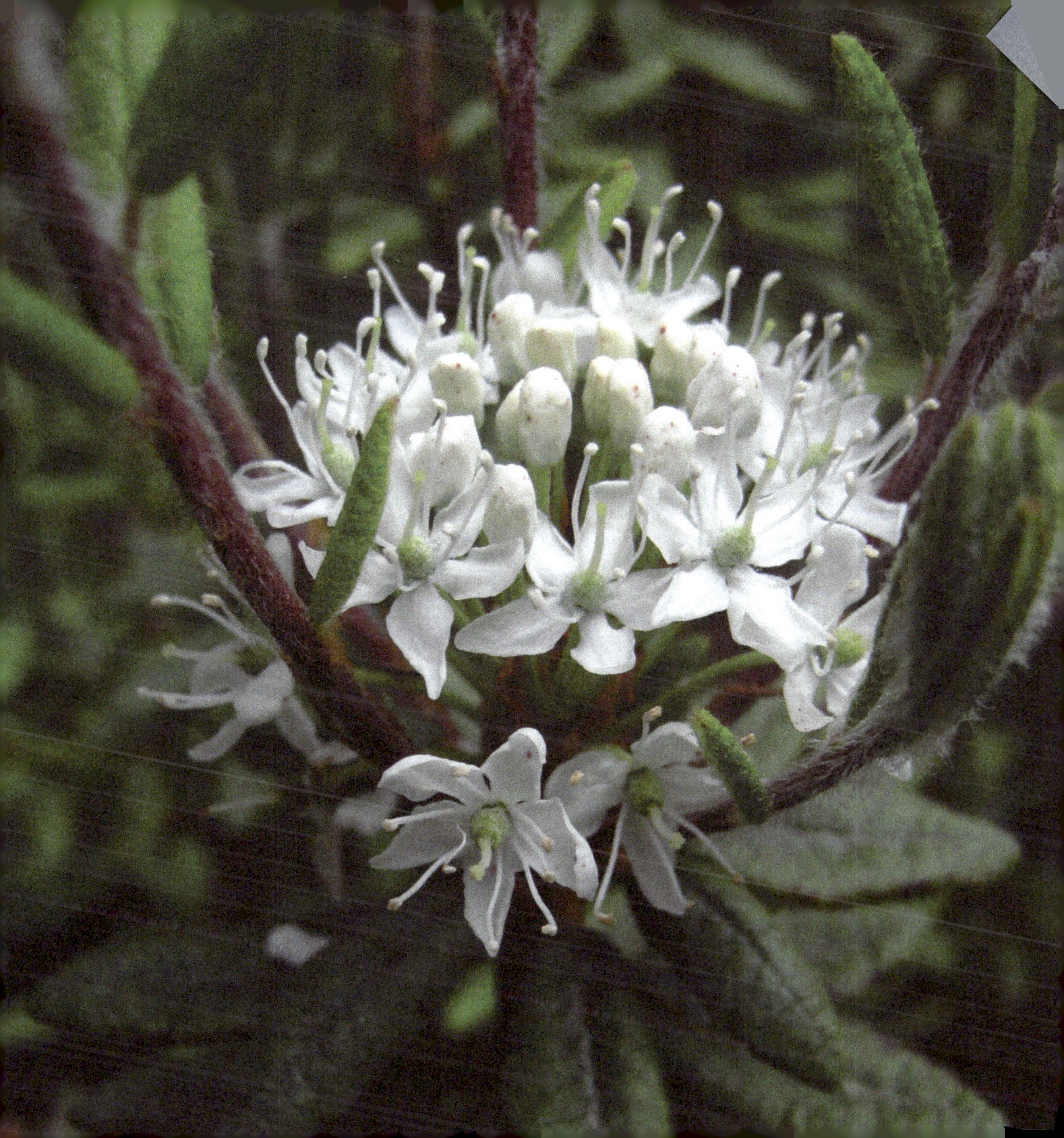

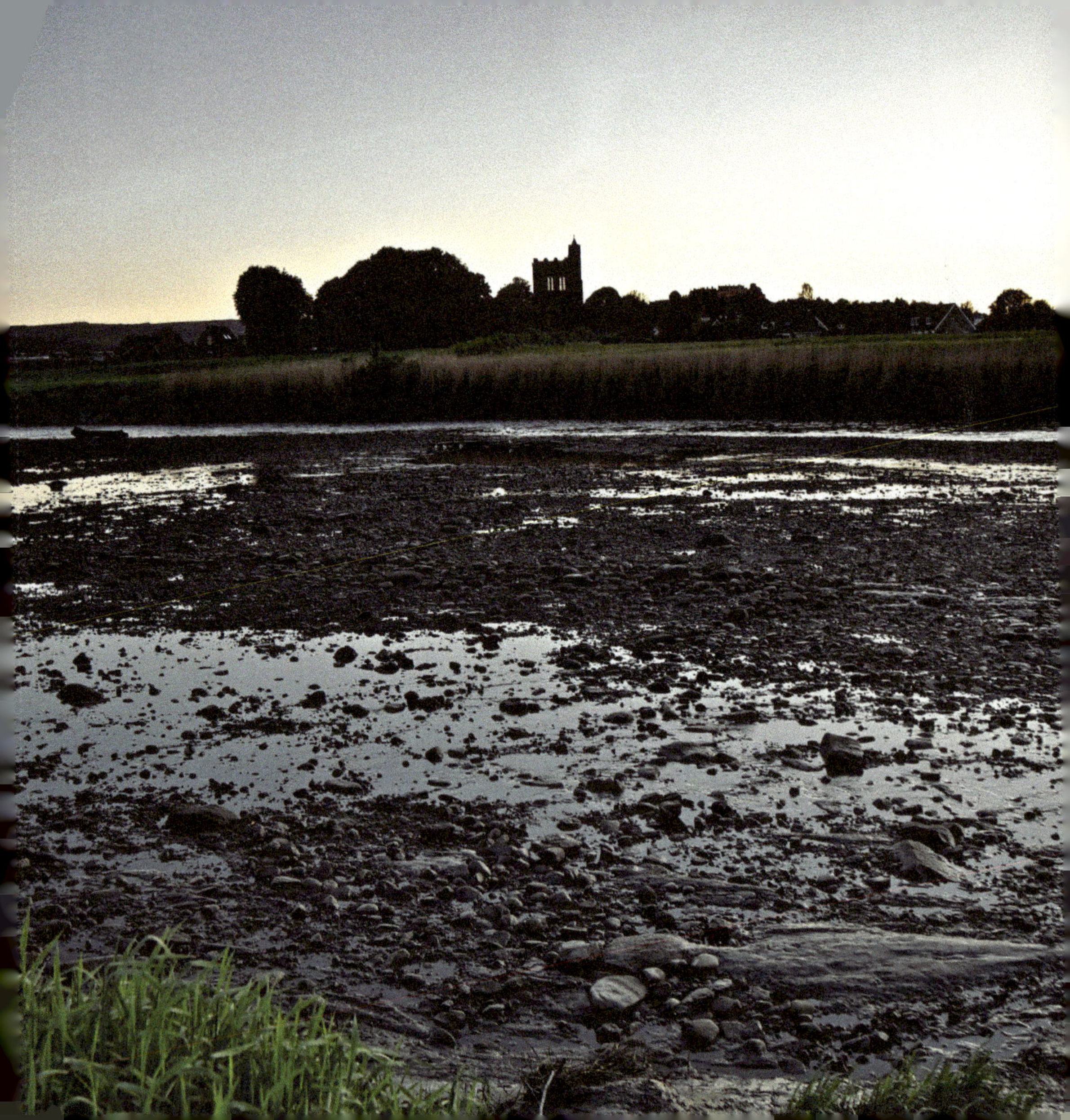

The Most Important Ford in Scotland

When you visit Stirling you will have to cross the Forth, which of course raises the question: how did people cross before the bridge was built? I know from personal experience that there is only one place to cross the river dry shod across its whole length: the Abbey Ford at Cambuskenneth. This was used from at least 2500 BC, and comprises a 500m stretch of bedrock and gravel. It's been used by thousands of people including Romans and Celts, Kings and Queens, and even the treacherous Earl of Atholl on his murderous midnight raid on the abbey during the Battle of Bannockburn. This was where brave Sir William of Airth was guarding the Bruce's baggage train and Atholl massacred him and his men. It is clearly the most important crossing point in Scotland—before Stirling Bridge was built.

The ford was probably the main reason David I gave the land to the Abbey in the 12th century, and it was probably he who built the first Stirling Bridge: the one that was destroyed during the Battle of Stirling. However, by the 16th century and after the Reformation—when the Abbey was demolished—the ford was becoming a nuisance, as larger and larger ships were being used and they struggled to get past the ford's rocks. So, periodically the burgh paid for people to clear the stones; for example, in 1610 every house in the whole town was to send a man for a day to clear the ford. In February 1727, the Council (or Burgh as it was) paid one William Henry Allan six pounds to measure it, and by 1777 there was a large 500 yard long channel cut through it. Despite all of this, the ford is still there and visible at low tide... though please don't try to use it. The mud is thick, and the tide's as treacherous as Atholl.

NS 81001 93926

Homes for Heroes

Blink and you will miss this. In the middle of a post-war housing estate, what looks like a drive without a car: it's full of poppies, and the gate says 'How Sleep The Brave'. On the side of the wall is a small white plaque. This is a war memorial without names to the fallen, as it commemorates and celebrates the survivors. It marks the construction of four cottages built on land supplied by Stirling Council for veterans of World War II. They were opened by the Earl of Rosebery in March 1947, who said there was now a greater emphasis on building homes for living veterans rather memorials for the dead. The ceremony also linked these current veterans to those who fought in The Battle of Bannockburn. The whole event was accompanied by a guard of honour from the castle led by Captain David Boyle, which was inspected by the Earl.

I think Captain Boyle's father was Colonel David Boyle, whose dad had been an Argyll and Sutherland veteran from World War 1 and the commander of the regiment. If three generations of service was not amazing enough, there is a sobering recording of Colonel Boyle in The Imperial War Museum's archive describing his time on the Burmese death railways, his humiliation, his routine beatings, and ultimately the resilience of him and his men.

NS 79323 91361

ARGYLL &
SUTHERLAND
HIGHLANDERS
1939-1945
WAR MEMORIAL

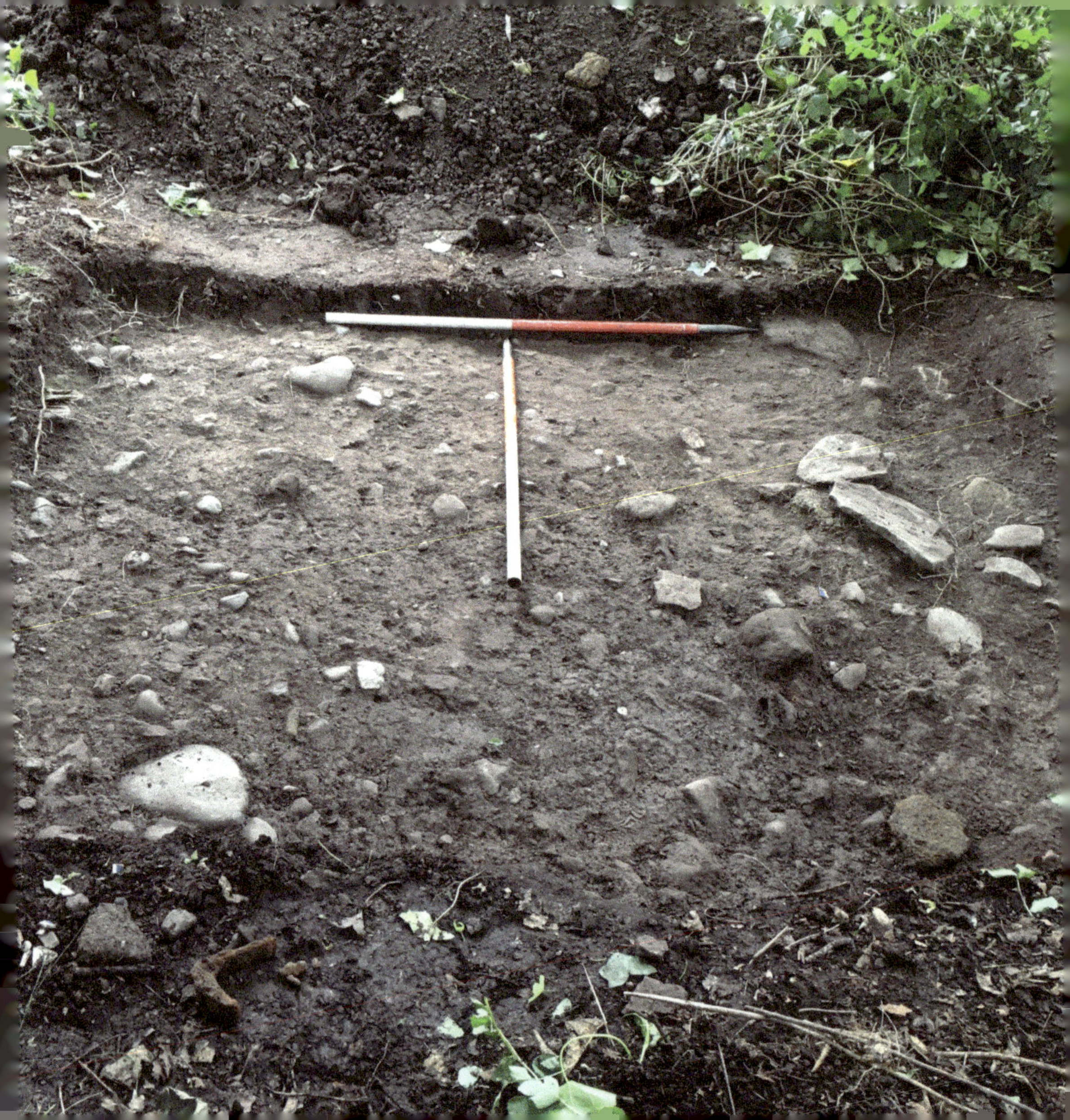

29
The Road to Destiny
The Sma' Folk of the Battle of Bannockburn

Let me be clear: I think Robert the Bruce was Scotland's greatest military leader, a man of genius and innovation, as well as being a rather ruthless killer. His greatest achievement—and Scotland's greatest ever victory—was the Battle of Bannockburn, which took place over two days and several locations. I think Bruce was playing chess, while Edward II simply imagined he could turn up and his greater numbers (at least a 2–1 advantage) would secure victory. Bruce planned both days: Day 1 did nothing but set the scene for Day 2; it forced the English from the main road to a boggy backwater, where Scotland's landscape and the clammy embrace of the Forth's wetlands would secure Scotland's freedom.

This is where the Sma' Folk come in. The name refers to their status in society; they were the common people and swarmed to Bruce's side, ensuring that he commanded his biggest ever force. They were stationed in the medieval New Park, the main surviving feature of which was a Cockshot Wood (the oldest in Britain). Tradition has it that when they witnessed that the English saw they were losing, they charged the battlefield. From the English perspective this looked like a new force; they would be caught in a pincer movement and utterly destroyed. And so they panicked and lost all discipline, and a Scottish victory became a rout. This is exactly what Bruce needed; he could not allow a beaten English army to reach the castle, lick its wounds and start again. Eventually, he and his patriots would tire (like the Jacobites after Falkirk at Culloden). So the big question is, did Bruce plan the Sma' Folk's attack? I say yes, and this small section of road I uncovered is where I think they marched to victory!

NS 78842 91747

A Lost Cemetery

The Cairn in The Kings Park

One of Stirling's most overlooked gems is the Kings Park, established in the 12th century as a mixture of hunting, farming and pleasure grounds. The southern boundary comprises a 2m high wall to keep deer in. This wonderful wall has a series of kinks and curves in it and, as will be revealed, these are connected to hunting deer. But there was also something else at play. If you look at the Royal Park from the Castle, the dyke vanishes behind the cliff and—like an infinity pool—you cannot see the edge. This makes it look bigger, and the Royal Park appears to extend to the horizon. This, of course, was designed to impress visitors to the castle of the power and prestige of the Scottish Crown.

Scotland's medieval monarchs were also interested in confirming and reaffirming that we were independent from England. Now, this might seem obvious, but English Kings tried to claim they were descended from the legendary King Arthur and so were the senior royal family. So how did we respond? Well, of course, we 'found' our own links to Arthur. As an aside, the first real person to be called Arthur was linked to Aberfoyle, and the earliest reference to King Arthur is in a poem composed about an army raiding Catterick from Edinburgh—so those links are there, though they needed sexing up! Stirling was called Snawdon (in reality a link to Snowdonia) and linked to King Arthur, and we had a Round Table (under what becomes the King's Knot). In recent years I've been working on a lost 4,000 year old cemetery (an 8m diameter artificial mound) in the Kings Park, right next to one of these bulges in the dyke. It looks like the dyke builder preserved the mound. Was this perhaps to provide another link to Arthur, as the King hunted deer?

NS 78566 92792

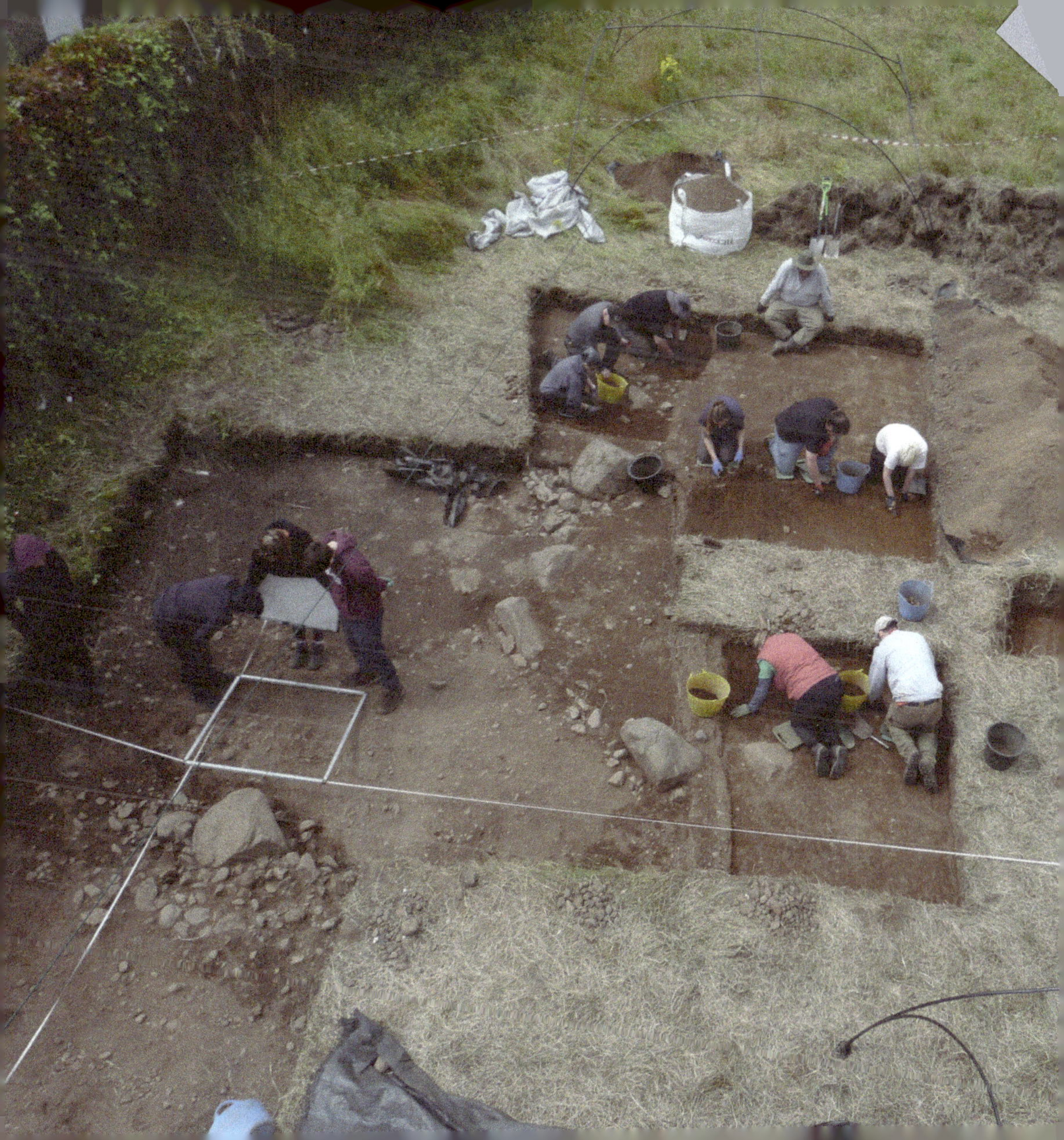

14 in.

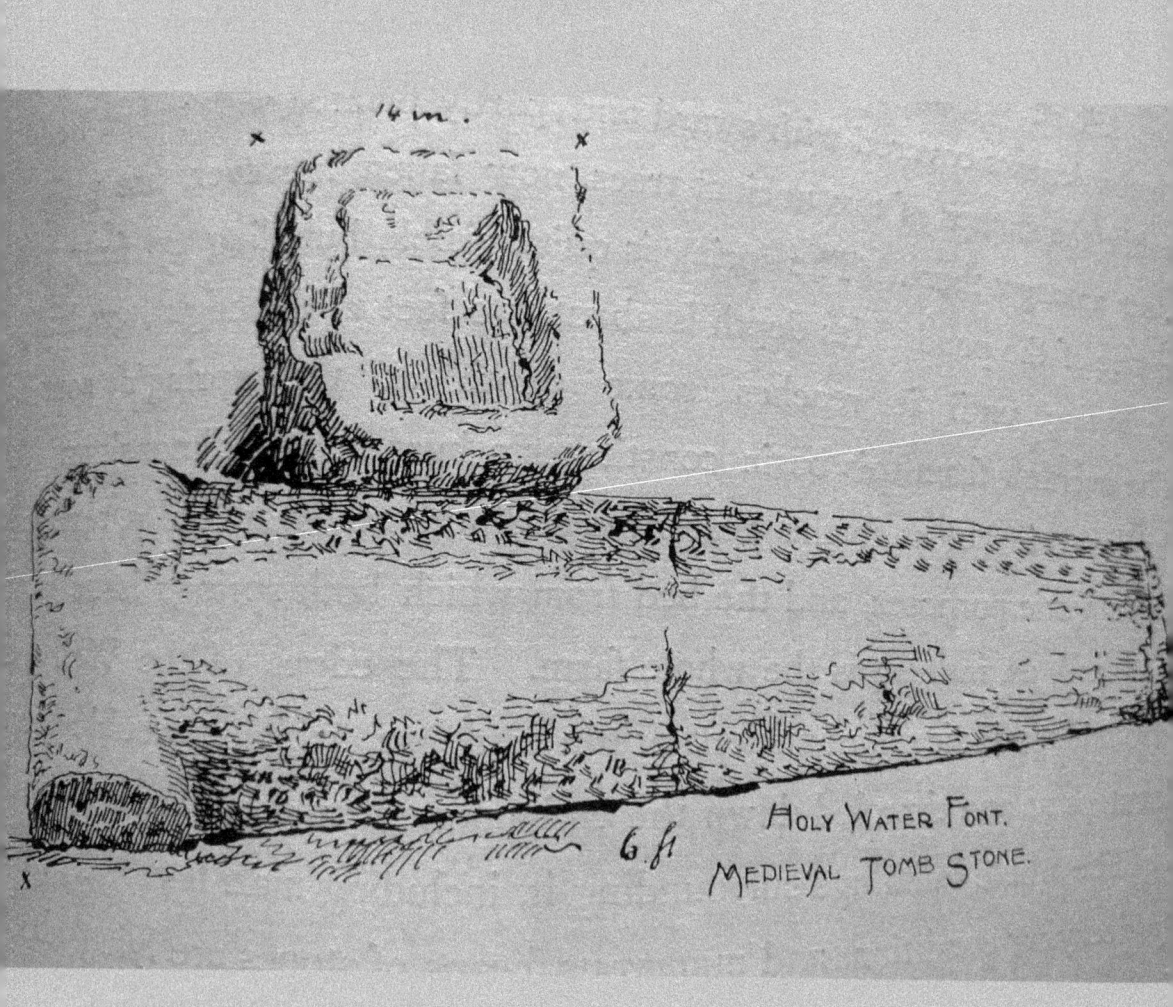

6 ft

HOLY WATER FONT.
MEDIEVAL TOMB STONE.

Stirling's Lost Hog-Back

Hogbacks are stone burials; monuments dating to the 10th to 12th century, and often linked to Viking or Norse influence (but it's a little more complex). The best examples look like long houses. On paper, Stirling has up to five: four at Logie Old Kirk, and one at St Thomas's Well in Cambusbarron. Vikings round Stirling, I hear you cry? Yes. The area was likely raided after the Battle of Dollar in 875, and Dunblane may even have been burnt down by Vikings around 917 (although the evidence for this may also refer to Dublin). The risk was real, and—as late as 1263—extra guards were mounted at Stirling Castle to watch for raids from Loch Lomond by the King of Norway around the Battle of Largs.

The St Thomas's Well example is just round from my house, so I went for a look. While it was noted by local antiquarian J.S. Fleming in 1898, it wasn't found in 1969 when someone else went to look for it. So I started hunting: I looked in stone dykes and knocked on doors, and once I spent a morning looking through a collapsed wall, all to no avail. My colleague John Harrison indicated there was no antiquity to the St Thomas name, there never was a church there, and that—worst of all—Fleming may have been on occasion a little too enthusiastic with his identifications. Hmm. And his drawing (opposite) shows a tapered stone with a 'T' end, which looks odd and definitely not very hogback! My conclusion was therefore that Stirling never had a fifth hogback. Still, I had fun finding out—and remember, there are definitely four at Logie (NS 81533 96972)!

No location, as it's lost!

Trial By Combat
Bruce's Well

The next five tales are designed to be read together as a walk. Start in Cambusbarron and walk to Bruce's Well, and follow the burn to Raploch. There is a path all the way, though it is a bit overgrown and muddy in places. This becomes a lade at some point—an artificial water course designed to feed a watermill; in this case the Bridge Mill. From Bruce's Well, walk east and then turn right onto The Brae, then left onto Mill Road past Hayford Mills and then right onto the path (NS 77450 92844). Head up the bank and over the road to Falleninch Farm (NS 77852 93623) and the path continues to Raploch Fire Station (NS 78523 94154).

We all know that the Battle of Bannockburn was Bruce's greatest ever victory, but remember he was Catholic (everyone was) and had been excommunicated for the killing of his rival, the Red Comyn, under a flag of truce on holy ground, which even today is a very shocking, brutal act. So victory at Bannockburn was also a signal that God was on his side. I mean, how else could a smaller, less well-equipped army have beaten the mighty English forces?

Anyway, local tradition has it that Bruce was blessed ahead of the battle at Cambusbarron at a small well on the Raploch Burn, which rises on the slopes of Gillies Hill. The well was associated with a mysterious chapel, which has completely vanished—though it's not clear that it was there during the War of Independence. The well was sealed in the 19th century following 54 deaths linked to the water, as it had been contaminated by open sewers in Cambusbarron. So please don't wet your whistle!

NS 77811 92518

Chapel Well
Cambusbarron

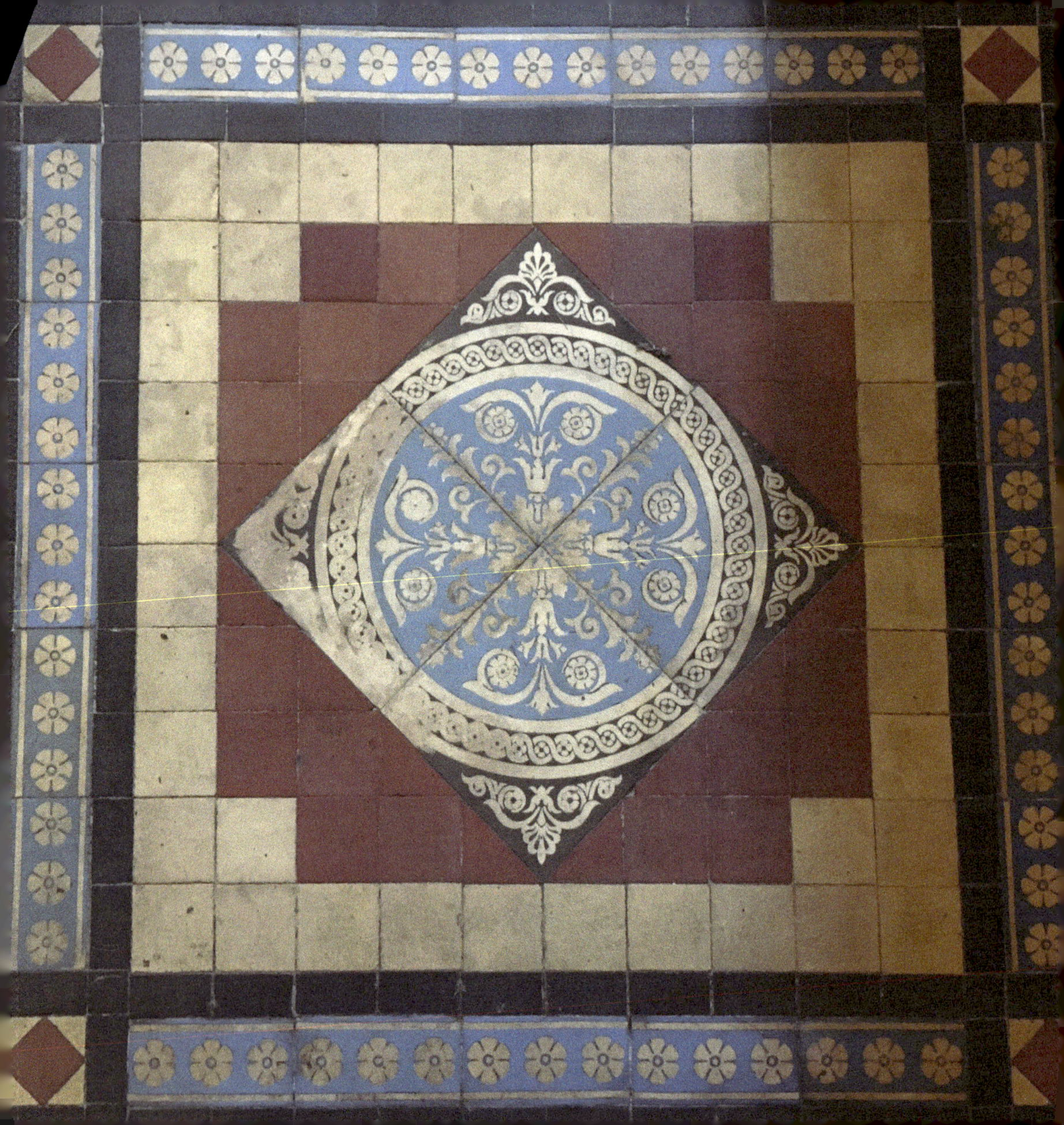

From Cambusbarron to Gallipoli
Hayford House and Mill

Hayford Mills, the largest factory in Stirlingshire, employed over 1,200 people, is made from multi-coloured bricks and is one of the most impressive Victorian buildings in Stirling; certainly the biggest! One of the later owners, Robert Smith, built the lovely listed Hayford House, but in October 1896, during his son's ownership (Robert Smith Junior), the mill went bust and the majority of Cambusbarron endured a miserable Christmas. The picture shows a detail of the ornate threshold mosaic, where Smith Senior entered in triumph and Smith Junior left dejected and miserable.

But our story concerns World War I, when the Lowland 52nd Brigade were billeted in the factory. One of the constituent battalions was to have a terrible war. The 1/7th Royal Scots, from my home town Leith, were involved in the worst rail disaster in British history. On 22nd May 1915 there was a signalling mistake, and over 200 people died; the precise death toll was never confirmed, as some bodies were never recovered. The bodies included four unknown children, who were never reported as missing. Half the soldiers died. The survivors were sent to fight at Gallipoli alongside the Anzacs.

Famously, the sea landings at Gallipoli were a total disaster (over 45,000 troops died). The campaign had been masterminded by Churchill, who was demoted after the debacle and said to a friend, 'I am finished.' He then resigned from government and volunteered to fight on the front. As an aside, the organiser of the disastrous sea landings, General Sir Ian Hamilton, who would later become a proponent for appeasement with Hitler, is buried just outside Doune at Kilmadock (NN 71674 00687).

Hayford House is a private dwelling, but the mill has been turned into flats so you can look at their wonderful, vibrant exteriors.

NS 77578 92862

The Oldest Functioning Lade
and Aqueduct in Scotland

As you leave Hayford Mills behind you, the carse begins to open up and—in due course—there is a low wall. This is corner of the Royal Park. Famously, Stirling has the oldest and best-preserved Royal Park in Scotland, founded in the 12th century by William I. Royal parks were intended to feed and entertain the Royal family and were a mixture of garden, park, farm and estate. Stirling actually has two of them: the Old and the New Parks (but very little survives of the New Park). Stirling's Old Park featured a golf course used by James IV, a fish pond, jousting grounds, an orchard, archery butts, deer dykes and formal gardens. It underwent a radical change around 1500 AD when James IV swapped the residential area, now called King's Park, for Gowan Hill as improvements in artillery meant that cannons could now fire upon Stirling Bridge, so it made sense to make the hill a military zone.

As you will see, a small stream runs to the west of the wall and it looks like the wall respects it, implying it's older. This is the lade for the medieval Bridge Mill. At one small low point, the water course is raised above the ground level—an aqueduct. Just think about that. This means that the lade, and thus the mill it fed, are at least 12th century in date. In other words, this water course was flowing when William Wallace won in 1297. Another little thing to note is this is also the boundary between the parishes of Stirling and St Ninians. We don't know when the parishes were formed, but all of this is likely to have been part of David I's plan for Stirling—the oldest functioning lade in Scotland. Wowser.

NS 77670 93265

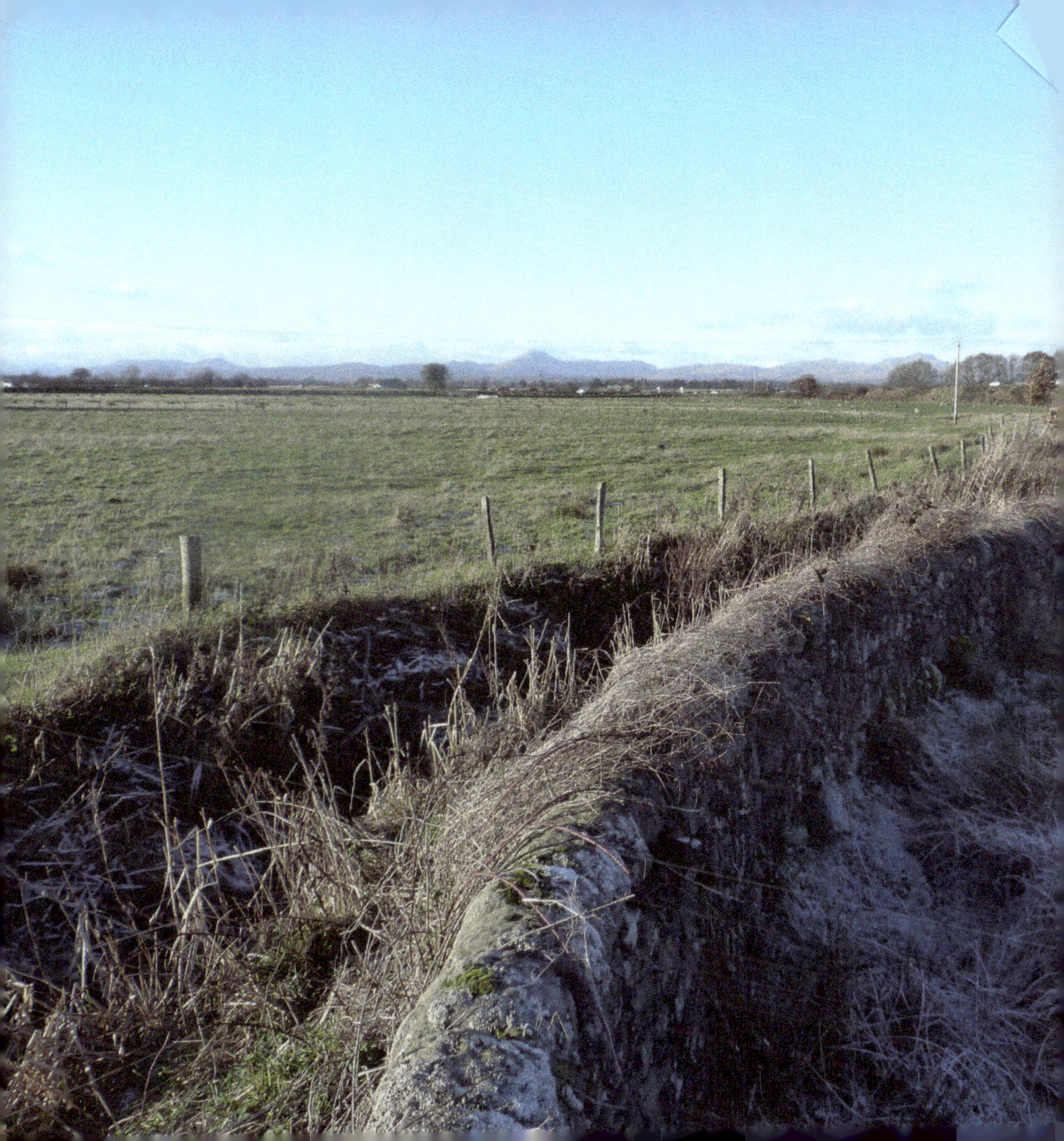

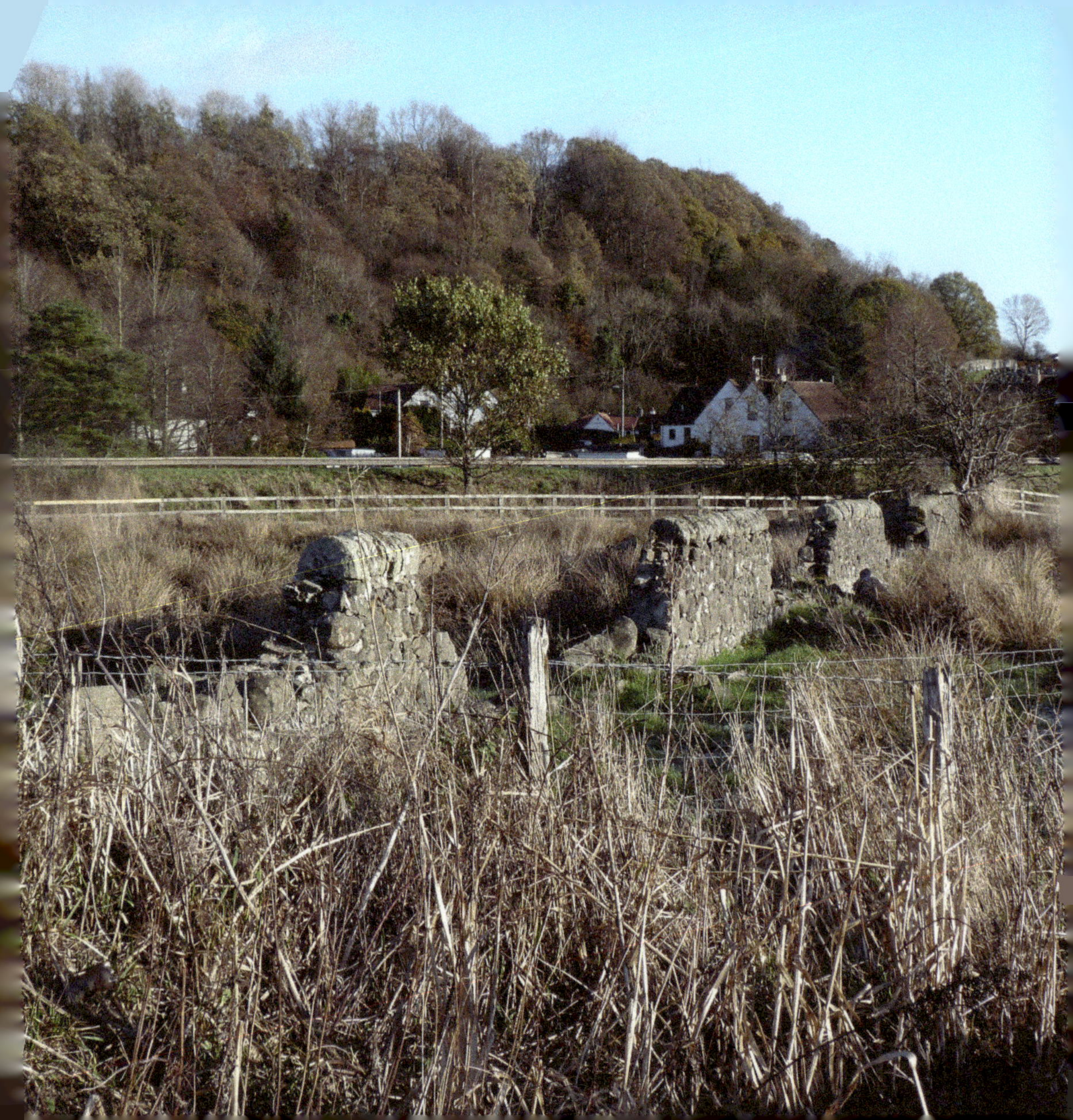

A Lesson From History
Always Keep an Eye on Contractors!

Now, as you're here, let's have another tale about the wall of the King's Park, which marks a nearly 900 year old boundary. Given its age, it's no wonder that the park boundary has changed a bit. The best preserved bit sits on the western section, is over 2m high, and has a series of very substantial stones as the top course rather than traditional coping stones. The wall was designed to stop deer jumping over it, and is the main reason why people think the Royal Park was only a deer park. Now, I know what you're thinking: if the best preserved bit is 2m high, why is this bit so scabby?

The wall was, obviously, built by subcontractors, and the thing with any subcontractor is that if you don't watch what they're doing you might get cheated. When I dug a section of the wall at The Homesteads, I found that the foundations were smaller. I used to think that they were cutting corners at the less visible bits, and this resulted in a 50% reduction of the wall with, no doubt, an inflated bill. But I now wonder if it was a deliberate design. As we've heard, the 2m high section runs to the south of a cliff and has a series of kinks and bulges that create pinch points. I think they probably fed the deer in the meadows created by the bulges, and the low walls let wild deer jump in. When it was time to hunt the deer, beaters would line the top of the cliffs and the deer would driven between the high walls and the beaters to the pinch points in order to be captured and butchered for the monarch's table.

NS 77670 93267

The Ten Aces from Raploch

In April 1916, a quiet field on Falleninch Farm below Stirling Castle was turned into a busy aerodrome known as Falleninch Field, or Raploch Aerodrome. The airmen lived in the farm and all the technical buildings were made of wood and canvas, all long since removed. A number of units were formed here or used the field, including No. 43, No. 63 and No. 77 Squadrons. The base was decommissioned after World War 1. The field saw the use of both the Sopwith Camel and Snipe—which are planes and not exotic beasties. Early on in the war, No. 43 Squadron (also known as the Fighting Cocks) moved on from the field and had a very distinguished history with ten Aces, each having downed at least five enemy aircraft. It ended up at Leuchars, Fife, and was finally disbanded in 2009.

Falleninch is an interesting name. 'Inch' is from the Gaelic word for island. We think that round Stirling, Gaelic was on the way out from the early 14th century, so this name is at least 700 years old. But why would someone call anything in this broad flat area an island? It's probably to do with a far older past. You remember the Bridge of Allan oyster bed? We know that as the sea retreated, the area to the west of Stirling was filled with large areas of bog, with dry cleared areas and routes. It's likely that the farm was built on such an area. Gradually, over time, the bog was cleared and the island vanished!

NS 78082 94026

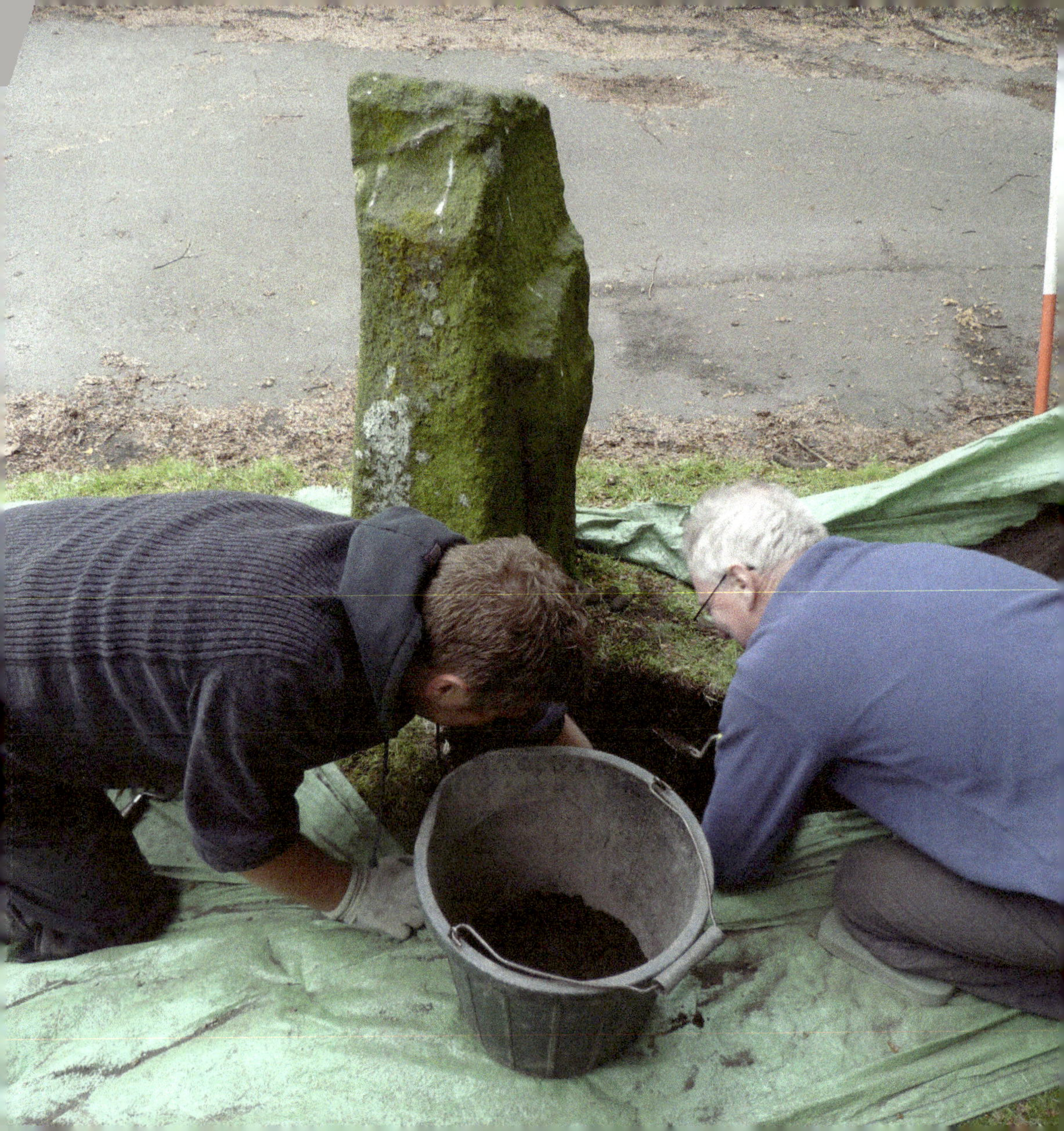

Stirling's Oldest War Memorial?

Given our strategic location, Stirling has been plagued by conflict for centuries. We are the most fought-over spot in Scottish history, and the very anvil of our national identity. All war memorials are worth reading, not just to remember the sacrifice and service of the fallen but also to think about the folly and greed of the aggressors. They become places of pilgrimage, respect and reflection for both sides of the conflict. However, what is likely to be Stirling's oldest war memorial is often ignored and lies at the side of a car park.

Two standing stones, only one of which is still in situ, lie in the grounds of Randolphfield House: now the local police headquarters. The house is named after Thomas Randolph, Earl of Moray; a Scot, who fought a successful skirmish against Sir Robert Clifford on Day 1 of the Battle of Bannockburn. Tradition has it that the stones were either here during the skirmish or perhaps erected in commemoration after it. I was sceptical (I always am): it was surely more likely that either these were prehistoric stones or perhaps even fake ones, erected in someone's garden as a joke? And so I did what I always want to do and dug a hole (with permission, of course; the police don't mess around!), and we found some charcoal that indicated that the one stone still in situ (the small one) had likely been erected at the time of the battle. Gosh, so perhaps Stirling's oldest memorial was erected in the immediate aftermath of victory in Scotland's most important battle? And yes, it's at the side of a car park (as mentioned), and every time I go past I say a little prayer, not just to the fallen but also that it doesn't get dunted by someone parking!

NS 79480 92499

St Ninians Tower
A Cradle of Christianity

An absolute requirement of any archaeologist is that they should be very nosy and curious. So I take every opportunity to poke my nose in every nook and cranny I can find. One of my favourite places to explore is St Ninians Church tower (and thanks to the Minister, Gary McIntyre, for letting me in); a brilliant place, reeking of history. The church saw Edward I ride from victory at Falkirk Bridge and his son flee in shame after Bannockburn. It was renovated by James IV and blown up by Bonnie Prince Charlie's troops. The tower may be around 900 years old, at which age it has already seen Christian worship for nearly 700 years, perhaps even as early as the late Roman Empire.

I was there to look at some older reused stones that had been built into the tower. But I took the opportunity to squeeze into the belfry and look at the magnificent brass bell which has the following inscription around it: *Such wond'rous powr to musick's given. It elevates the soul to heaven. Pack & Chapman of London Fecit 1774.* (*Fecit* is Latin for 'made it'.) The bell still chimes to this day, and the wooden frame that supports the bell is covered with generations of precise, tidy graffiti: etched names and dates. The oldest one is by Thomas Aitken and dates to 1774. The obvious conclusion is that Thomas erected the bell, or certainly helped with it. I can find nothing else on Thomas; one more name in a very long list of lives the tower has seen. What will its next 900 years bring?

Unfortunately at present neither the tower nor the graveyard at St Ninians Old Church is open to the public, but you can wander around its outside walls and gaze in.

NS 79583 91670

G.P. 1886

A.P.

D. HUGHE

H. STEWART
1954

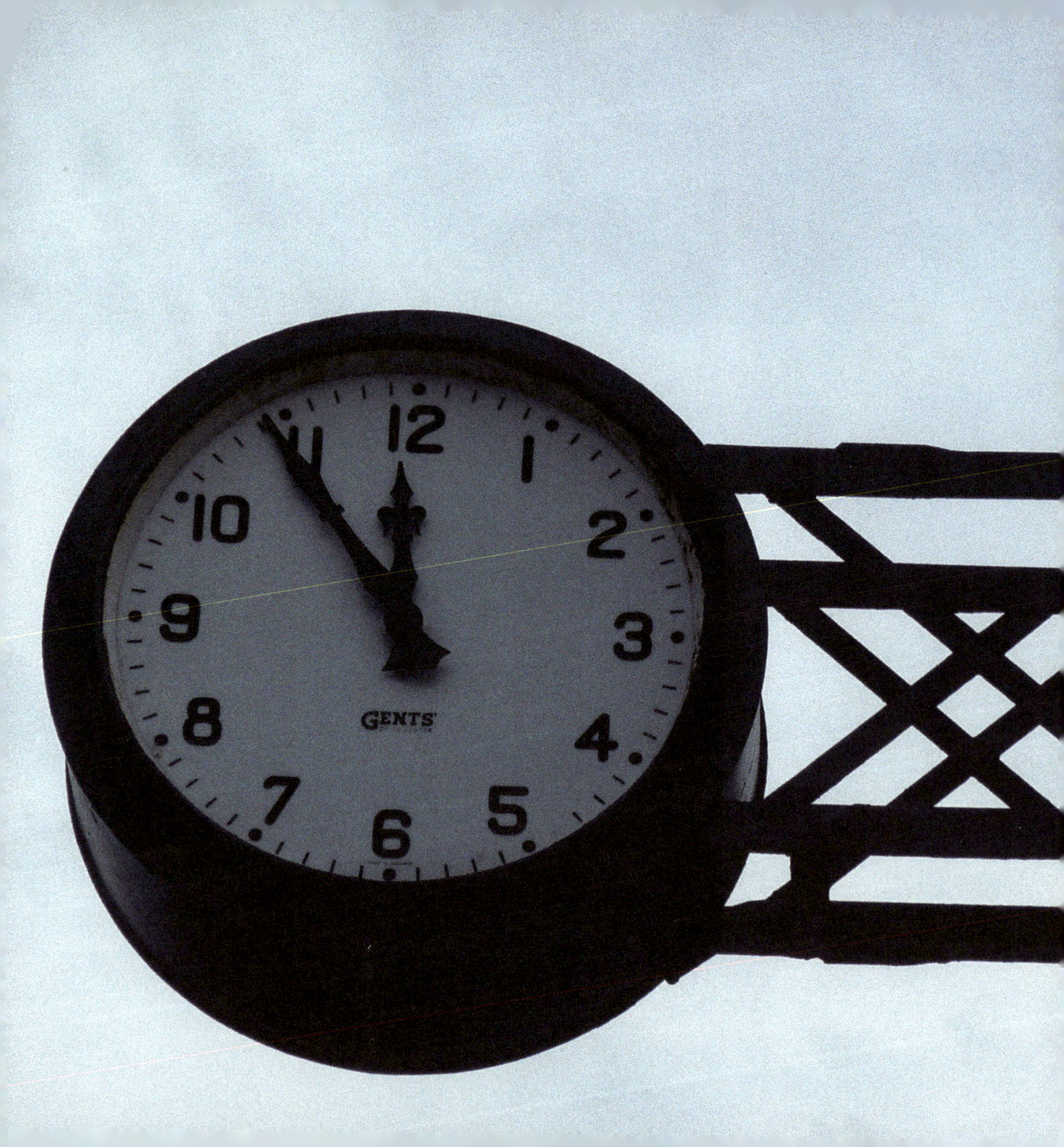
GENTS'

Clock Watching
for 132 Years and Counting!

In an anonymous business park to the east of Stirling train station lies the John Player Building. Above the main entrance hangs this clock designed by Gents of Leicester; a proud firm with a noble, century-long tradition of clock-making. It was there to make sure people worked their allotted hours. The complex started as a carpet factory in February 1890 which shut in the 1950s, as Australian markets closed after Britain joined the EU. In turn it became a cigarette factory, passing through various companies before becoming associated with John Player who were famous for their collectible cards. This closed in 1982, and the complex then became associated with small businesses. Thousands upon thousands of hours worked, ambitions realised and thwarted, lives lived in the happy monotony of a steady income.

The factory narrowly avoided been blown up in World War II when a German landmine intended for it hit the Kings Park football ground instead. The explosion left a smoking crater 18 feet deep and 40 feet wide. The blast radius of this bomb also damaged a row of houses, making several families homeless. The gunner in the bomber also took the opportunity to strafe the town with machine gun fire and spent shells, and bullets were found across the town. One bullet even embedded itself in a church pillar. Rather bizarrely, the bomb blew the door on a nearby joiner's shop off its hinges, while the windows remained intact. The impact to the joiner's reputation is not recorded, but presumably the glazier enjoyed a surge in sales! And in what must surely be a morale boosting tall-tale: a goldfish's tail was blown off and the wee fish was revived from the shock by a few drops of brandy.

NS 80232 93160

From Top to Bottom

Exploring Bannockburn House

One of the many great things about Scotland is the support for community buy-outs, where local people get to buy and manage important buildings and landscapes. The most impressive example in Stirling is the wonderful 17th century Bannockburn House, which hosted Bonnie Prince Charlie—twice. He survived an assassin's bullet and plotted the last-ever siege of Stirling Castle, as well as meeting his lover Clementina Walkinshaw (whose child was the only one of his to survive infancy), under its roof. The house is now run by the local community and is well worth a visit.

As the Council's Archaeologist, I was asked to help out a few times and was only too happy to assist. Anyway, in the early days I took full advantage and wandered everywhere—even into places I really shouldn't have gone, and you can't go, due to asbestos and rotten floor boards.

Anyway, I found my way to a basement down some very narrow cold stone steps, the light from our mobiles casting strange shadows. The ceiling had several rusty hooks for storing butchered carcasses (animals not people!). Unfortunately for me, I had been talking about *The Blair Witch Project* and how the basement reminded me of the final scene… I frightened myself and gave a piercing scream! With the guffaws of my friend echoing, we then went to the attic—another forbidden place. There we found Roman numerals and spiky pegs. The numerals were probably to do with the Baltic timber trade, where most of Scotland's 17th century timber came from, but what were the pegs? These were wooden oak dowels used to secure the roofing tiles. When they were replaced by slates, they were knocked down from the outside! I went again more formally and asked to take pictures for this book, and the trustees graciously allowed me back in. While I mentioned my first trip, I didn't mention the scream!

NS 80890 88908

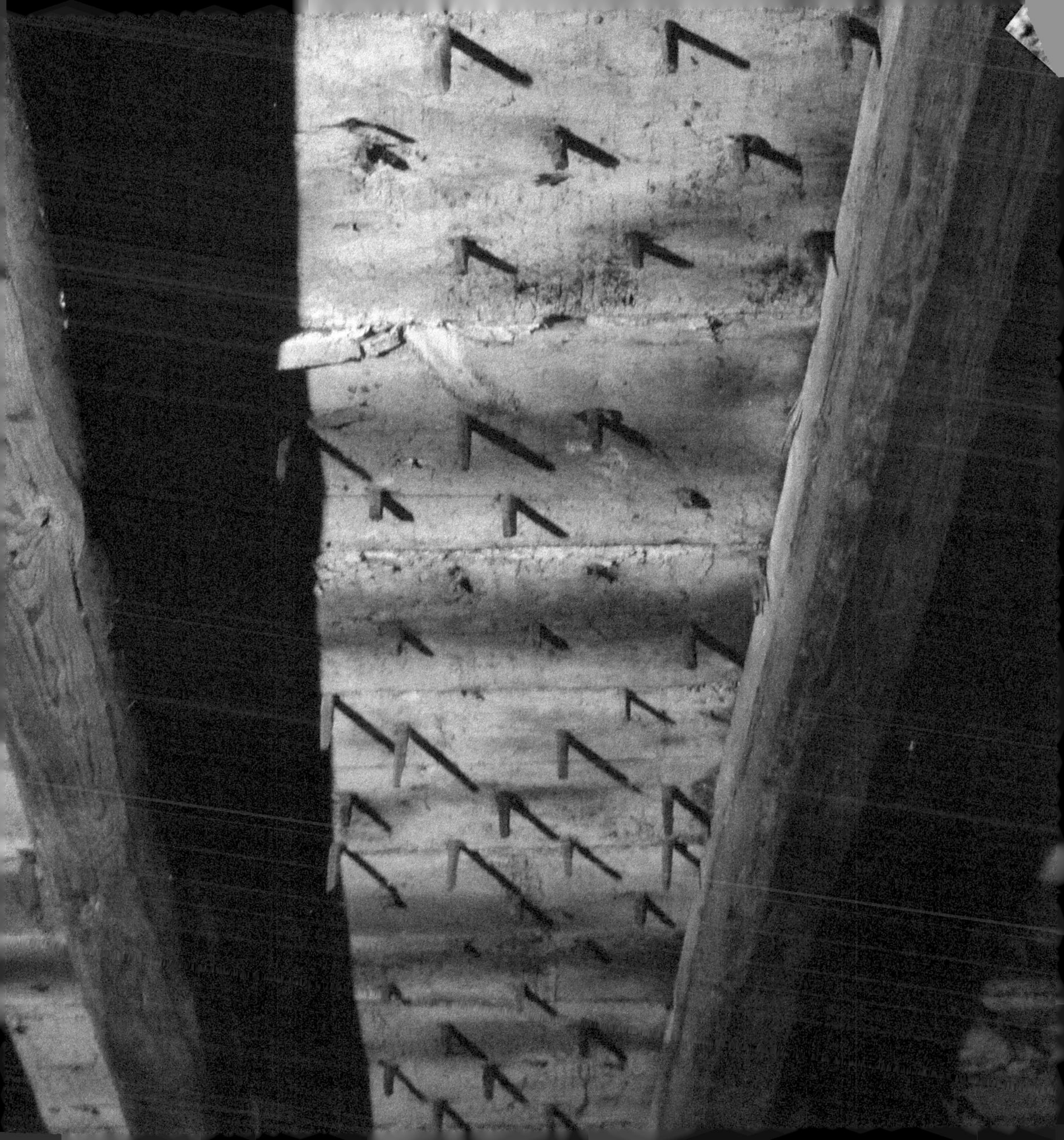

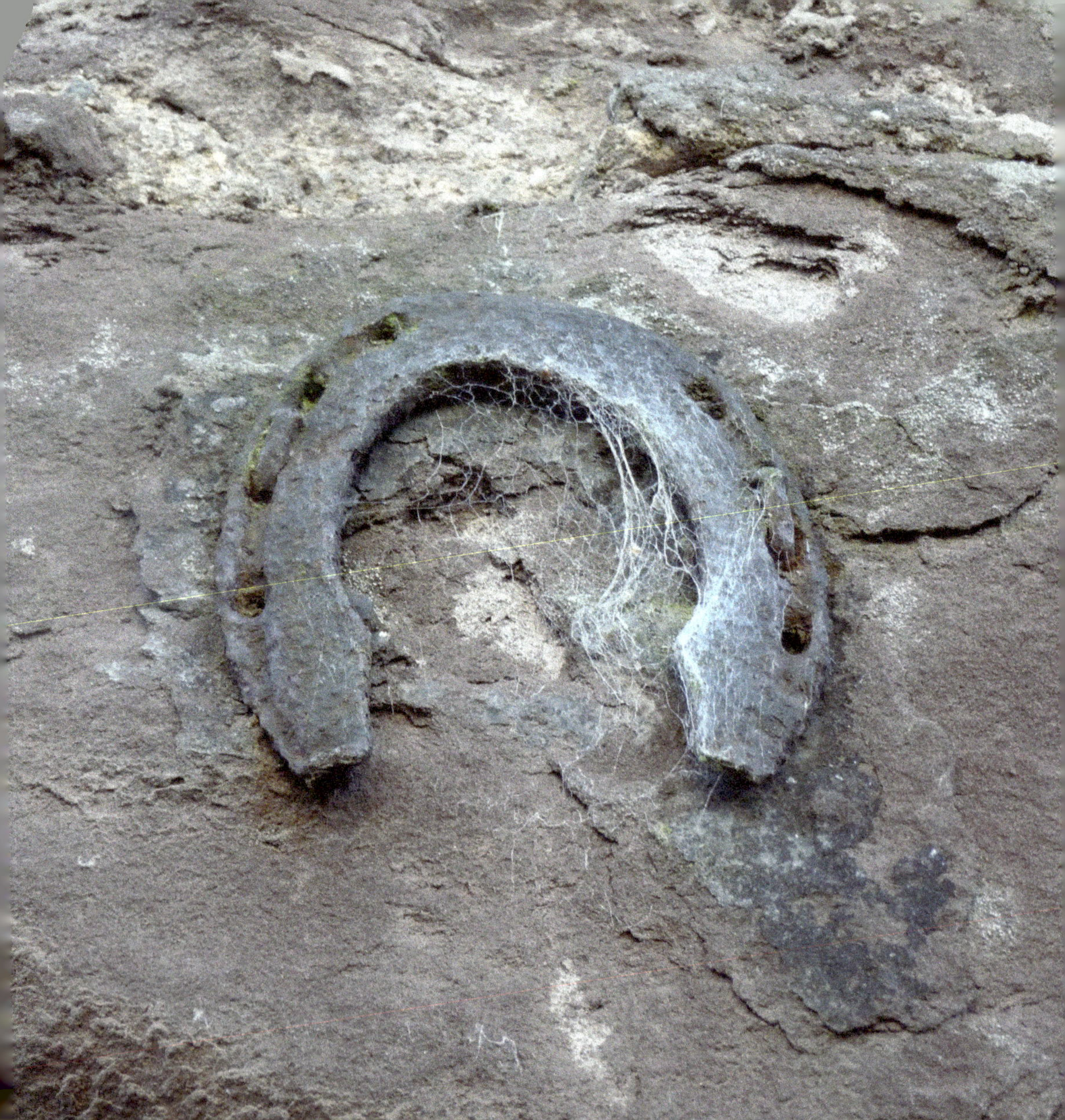

By Royal Appointment... Not!
Dunblane's Cheeky Blacksmith

Round Stirling. some people claim that Dunblane—and not Stirling—is Scotland's smallest city. (I know, the absolute cheek of it.) Now, of course, Dunblane has a cathedral and Stirling does not, but we do have a Royal Charter and a castle. And if we're playing that game—Dunkeld is only a tenth of the size, so there.

Dunblane has its own royal connections, as well as two not-bad tennis players. The first of the connections is King Aed, the son of King Kenneth MacAlpin and infamously the last man to be known as the King of the Picts. Aed took power in the face of fierce Viking raids, and was eventually murdered by his retainers in what would become Dunblane. The Pictish Kingdom collapsed in a mixture of internal strife and invasion, and the country rebranded itself to Alba. Who knows: if Aed had a been bit more canny, perhaps we would still be called Picts? The second is far more contentious and involves Edward I, who stripped the lead off the Cathedral to build the War Wolf—the world's largest trebuchet, which was used in the siege of Stirling Castle in 1304.

Dunblane's third royal connection, and the point of this story, is with Queen Victoria. On the 13th September 1842, Victoria and Prince Albert were travelling through the village when one of the horses pulling the Royal Carriage lost a shoe. A local blacksmith, one Mr McKenzie, repaired the damage and kept the remains as a souvenir. The broken horseshoe was nailed to the wall and a crown carved into the wall, and he claimed to be by royal appointment. Queen Victoria's thoughts are not recorded—though we suspect she might not have been amused!

NN 78154 01029

Scotland's Heart

Where exactly is the heart of Scotland? Now, I don't mean our emotional core that beats rapid and fast when our various national teams compete and fail (though we did win the world elephant polo once) or flutters at the merest hint of a bagpipe—or should that be a deep fried pizza? No, I mean the geographical core. This has changed over time: so not before c.1100 when the Lothians were part of Northumbria, and not before 1263 when Norse influence in the west ended at the Battle of Largs, but after 1469 when the northern isles once again became Scottish after Denmark ceded their rights as their Princess Margaret married the future King James III.

Lots of places claim to be central to our fair nation: the Harthill Services on the M8 (not the most romantic location) or perhaps Perth and Kinross Council? Well one man, Mr William Murdoch Esquire of Gartincaber House, disagreed with everyone (except local tradition) and decided that the centre of Scotland was close to him. And so with a remarkable confidence, he built a two storey gothic octagon tower in 1799 and let people visit it. The tower was described by the august Royal Commission on Ancient and Historic Monuments of Scotland as being 'built in sandstone rubble, with dressed stones at the corners and window and door surrounds... An iron spiral staircase wound around the outside of the tower and gave entry to the two storeys, defined by a dressed stone string course. Each floor had a fireplace. The crenellated parapet hid the flat roof, which supported a flag pole.'

In the 20th century it was used for secretive military purposes. The tower has suffered in recent years and was devastated by a storm in 2012 and all that now remains is a low wall.

NN 69763 00801

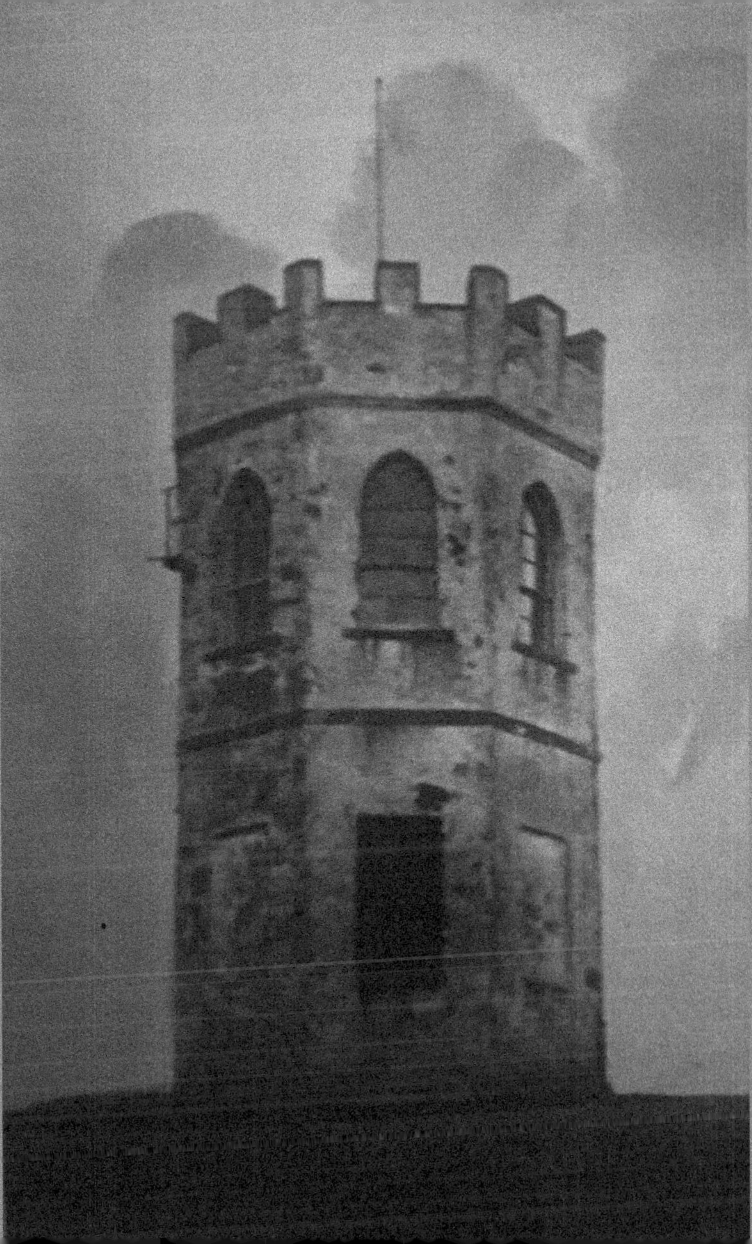

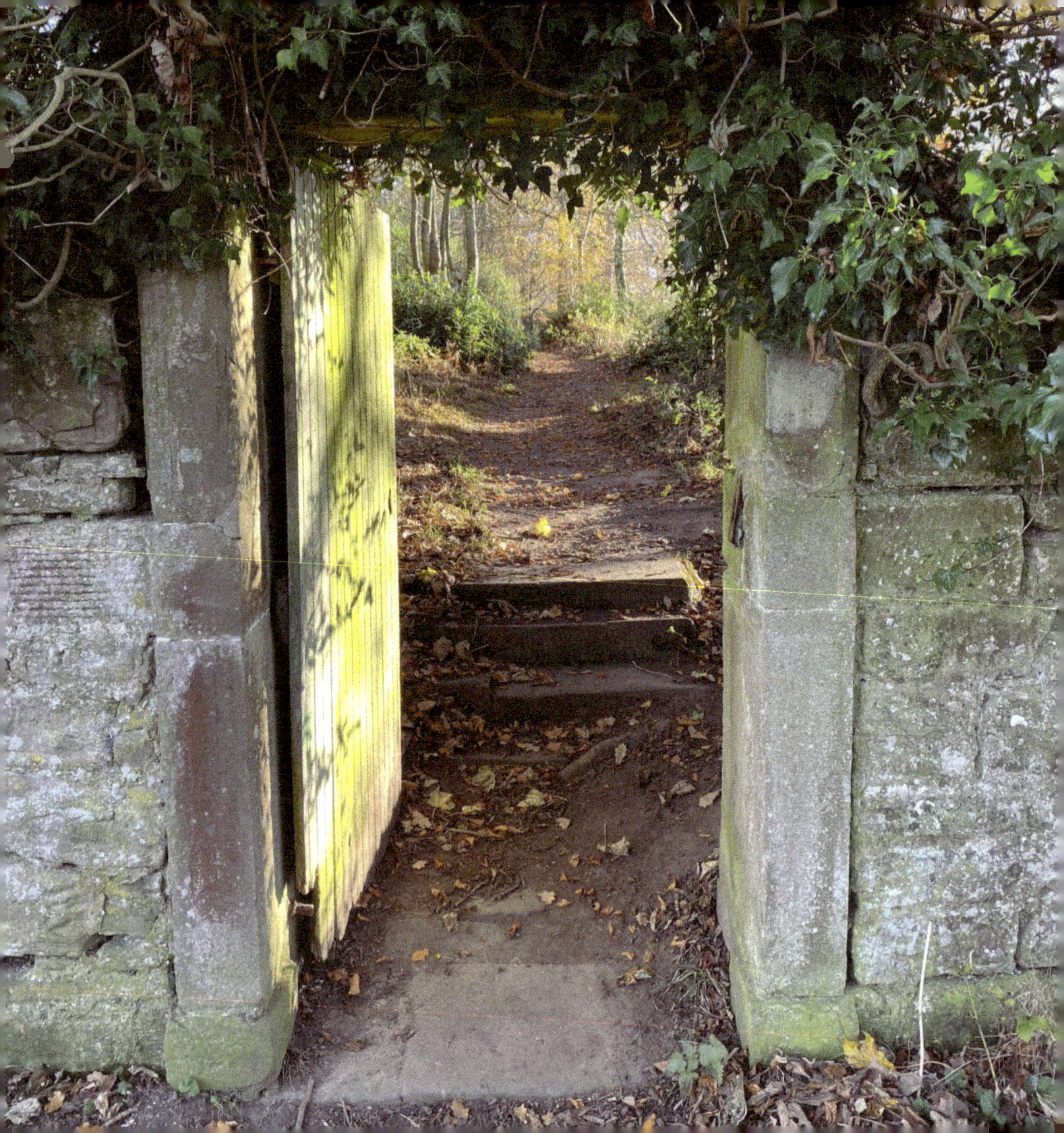

Christ's Well
Reformation and Repression

Scotland has had a number of religious revolutions over the centuries: our initial conversion to Christianity, and then the Reformation when we like to think we threw off outdated superstition for the logic and clear thinking of the Kirk. Previous generations viewed this as our gateway to success: the Union of the Crowns, then Parliaments followed, and in turn the Enlightenment and Empire. We traded the freedom of poverty for England's gold. The reformation came at a cost, though: Scotland in the late 16th and 17th centuries was a virtual theocracy. Christmas and Easter were banned, and we began to prosecute people for a non-crime... witchcraft.[5] In recent years, the role of the Kirk has dropped in Scotland, churches are being sold off at breakneck speed, and the passions and actions of the Reformation seem extreme, alien and odd.

So, let me take you to not just a secret location but one which was actually illegal. Christ's Well, in the grounds of the Blair Drummond estate, was considered an ancient holy well associated with healing. This was *verboten* as far as the Kirk was concerned and, from 1581 to 1643, local ministers tried to stop anyone taking the waters, praying or leaving gifts there, or even sprinkling the water on their cattle. People were accused of communing with the Devil, and their punishments included attending church in sackcloth and linen for three successive Sabbaths and a fine of £20 (nearly £3,000 today), or else face imprisonment! Yikes.

I got lost trying to find this and it was disappointing, but the walk is excellent, full of massive trees, red squirrels and best of all a fabby motte (NS 72472 98668). The picture is of the entrance to the estate from cemetery end, where you can park (NS 72097 98715).

NS 72920 98902

Stirling's Lost Roman Fort

Yeah, I know what you're thinking. How can you lose a Roman fort? Well, it's easy, and honestly we don't really know how many we originally had. Most things happen in Scotland in the same places: the roads, the towns, the population and the invasions all run in an arc around the east coast. So, we've already lost a fair whack of Roman activity.

In our case, it's the same broad argument but we put a coal mine and then a dump on ours! So let's start at the beginning. Two local metal detectors, Gordon Dunbar and the late Jim Dawson, had been hitting the maps and spotted a 'Roman Camp' on Stobie's 1783 map: The Counties of Perth and Clackmannan. No one else had spotted this, and it was unknown. The site features in the late 18th century Statistical Account for Alloa, where it is described as a 'small castellum' and is linked to a possible ford. The fort was right on the Forth, next to a dog-leg natural inlet from the Forth at this location, just before the major meanders of the river. Perhaps a natural harbour controlled by the Romans—double wowser! It's a great spot, and I even went for a swim (don't I always?).

Now, while Stobie will have spotted something, quite what is uncertain—and it's possibly not a fort; it could be a marching camp or a fortlet, or perhaps it's a native fortification rather than a Roman one. Anyway, we decided to have a look and the first thing we had to deal with was the 10 feet high toxic hogweed. So we went in the spring and cut a path through the new growth and then dug some holes—through tonnes of rubbish. No fort yet, but we've not given up... watch this space.

No location, as we don't really know where to go!

Northfield Bridgend
Maner
Roman Camp
Blackgrange
W.Cambus
Blackgrange haugh
Polmeas

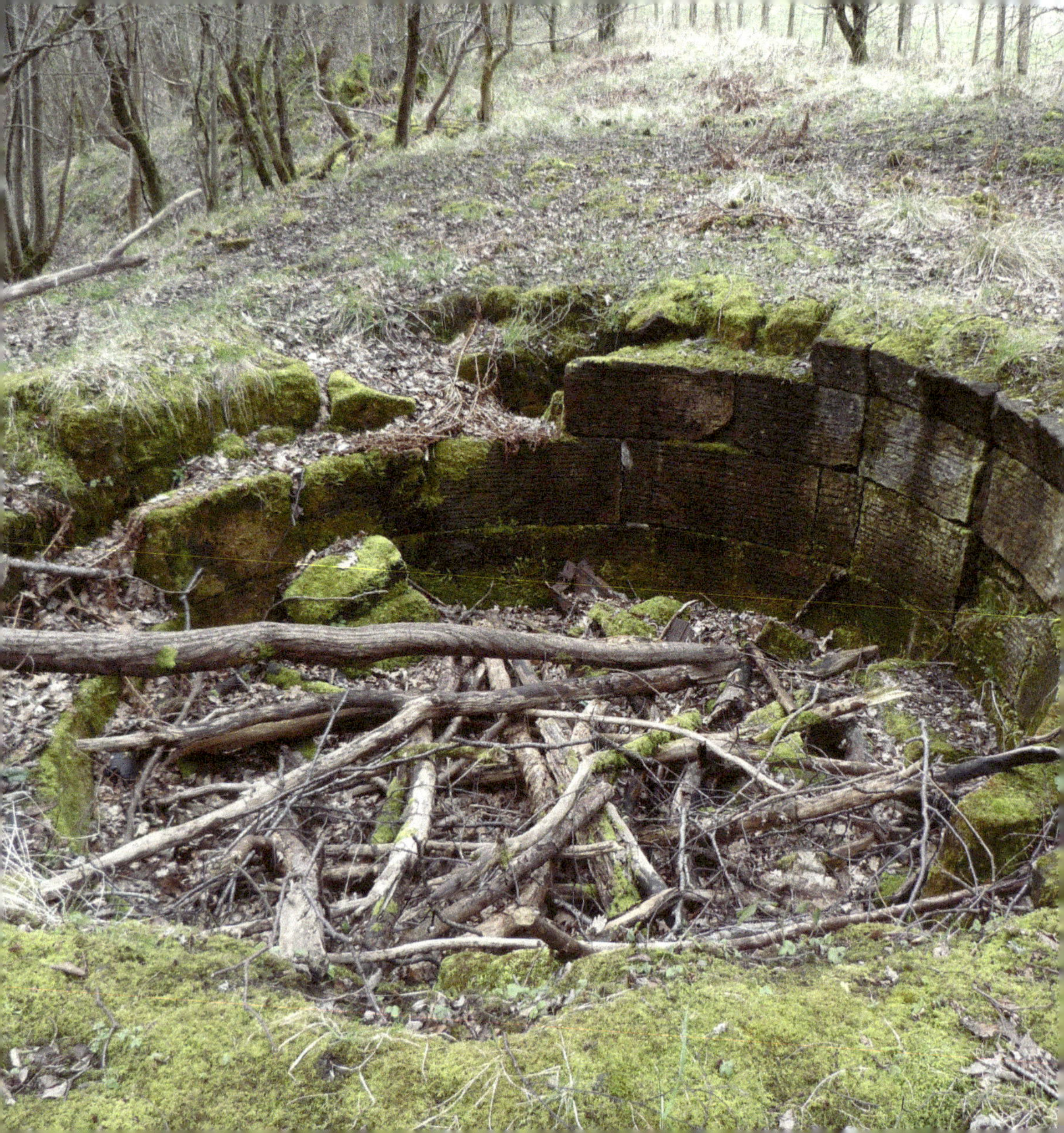

An Abandoned Freezer in Fallin!

Now, don't get the wrong idea; this is not a story about fly-tipping. You like ice cream, right, or perhaps a cold one from the fridge? Maybe, like me, you've got mysterious Tupperware at the back of the freezer containing leftovers no one wanted? We take all of this for granted, but it was once the preserve of the seriously rich. They cut ice from lochs in the winter and stored it in sunken chambers (ice houses) for the summer. Of course, it was the likes of you and I that did the cutting so the 1% could get their chilled G&T!

This is a lovely wee walk from Fallin over what was the original main road east-west. Make sure you look at the 18th century bridge, from which it's a brief saunter to the north. This broken hole is all that remains of the original 17th century Polmaise Castle and its estate. This was pulled down shortly after the family moved to Gillies Hill, and then that castle was blown up in the 1960s after a fire. The garden of this later one (NS 77762 91687) is being restored by the local community and is well worth a visit. Returning to Fallin, our 'freezer' would originally have had a domed roof (there is an upstanding one in Bridge of Allan at NS 79089 9761); you can see a wee gap between the two walls. This double wall acted to insulate the interior (like double glazing) and keep it cold through the summer. Things like this raise mixed emotions. I mourn the loss of fine architecture, but am quite pleased that no one is gathering ice for the privileged.

NS 83421 92286

Winding Up The Age of Improvement

Late 18th century Scotland saw one of the most remarkable increases of agricultural output in world history, as production increased by nearly 300%. This was achieved by the mechanisation and commercialisation of farming; irregular fields were expanded and squared off to make ploughing easier, and new crops were introduced. The turnip allowed farmers to keep herds of animals alive over winter. They previously had to kill them to eat and store as there was never enough winter fodder, which is why we had so many feasts between Autumn and early Winter (Halloween and Christmas!). This was, of course, the same drive that led to the Highland Clearances; generations of loyal Highlanders made less money than sheep, an absolute tragedy and on occasion a crime. But another action we might regret even more today, with the encroaching climate crisis, was the clearing of peat to create ever more farmland. Sometimes this was small scale, the individual actions of small tenants: The Moss Lairds. These people were given peppercorn rents if they cleared the peat; some even lived in peat igloos carved from that carbon-rich soil. When the land became fertile, the rent went up!

Of course, even small-scale actions—if repeated by hundreds of people over decades—had a big impact, and whole bogs have vanished. But this was not enough, and enormous mechanical pumps were used to drain the bogs and get rid the 'useless peat'! Sometimes, however, the peat might find a use—as was the case at Dunmore, where in the late 18th century this pump was used to manage the water level so that the peat might be gathered to help produce whisky. Now, however, much I like whisky I'd still rather have the peat!

NS 86147 89463

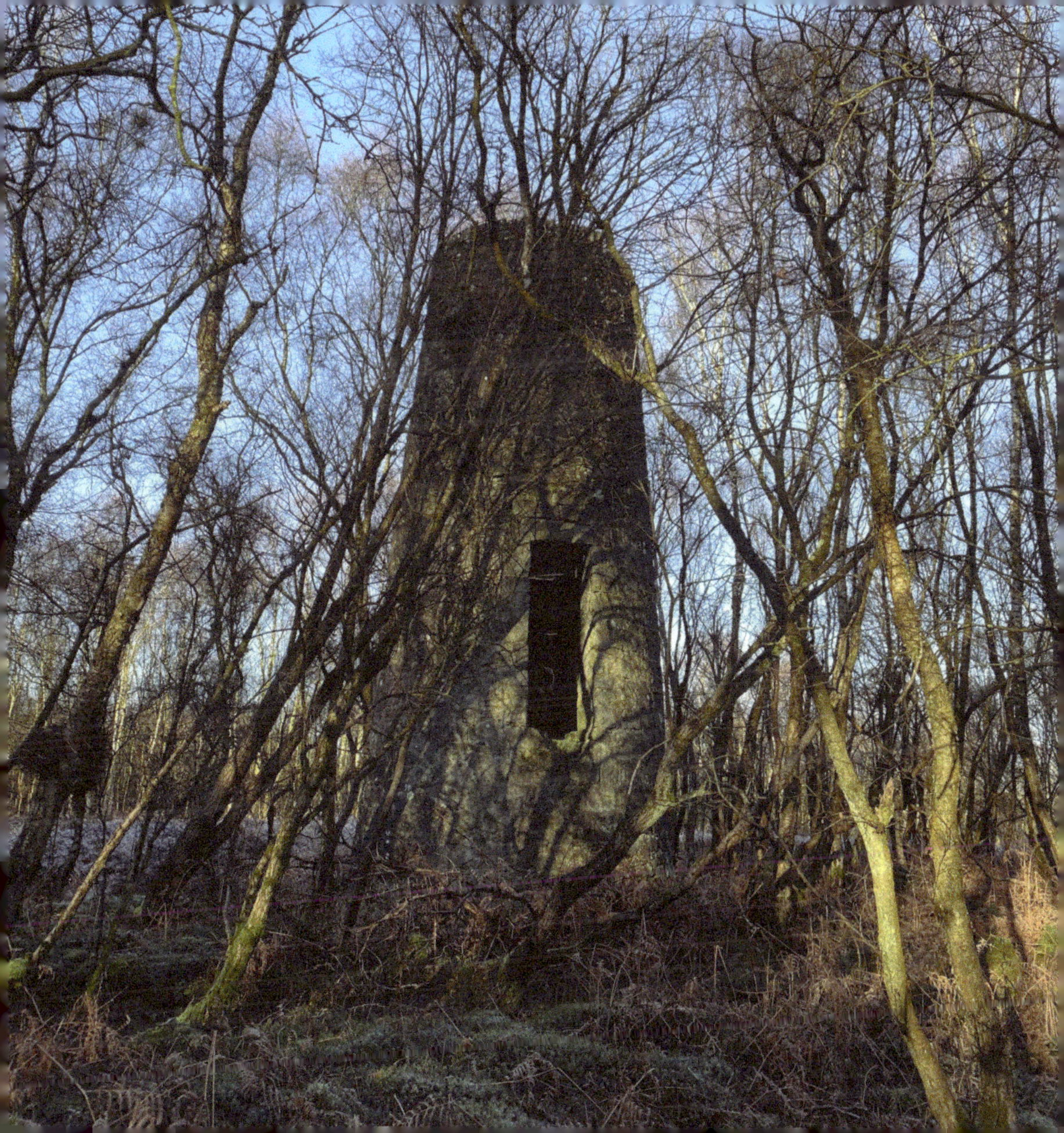

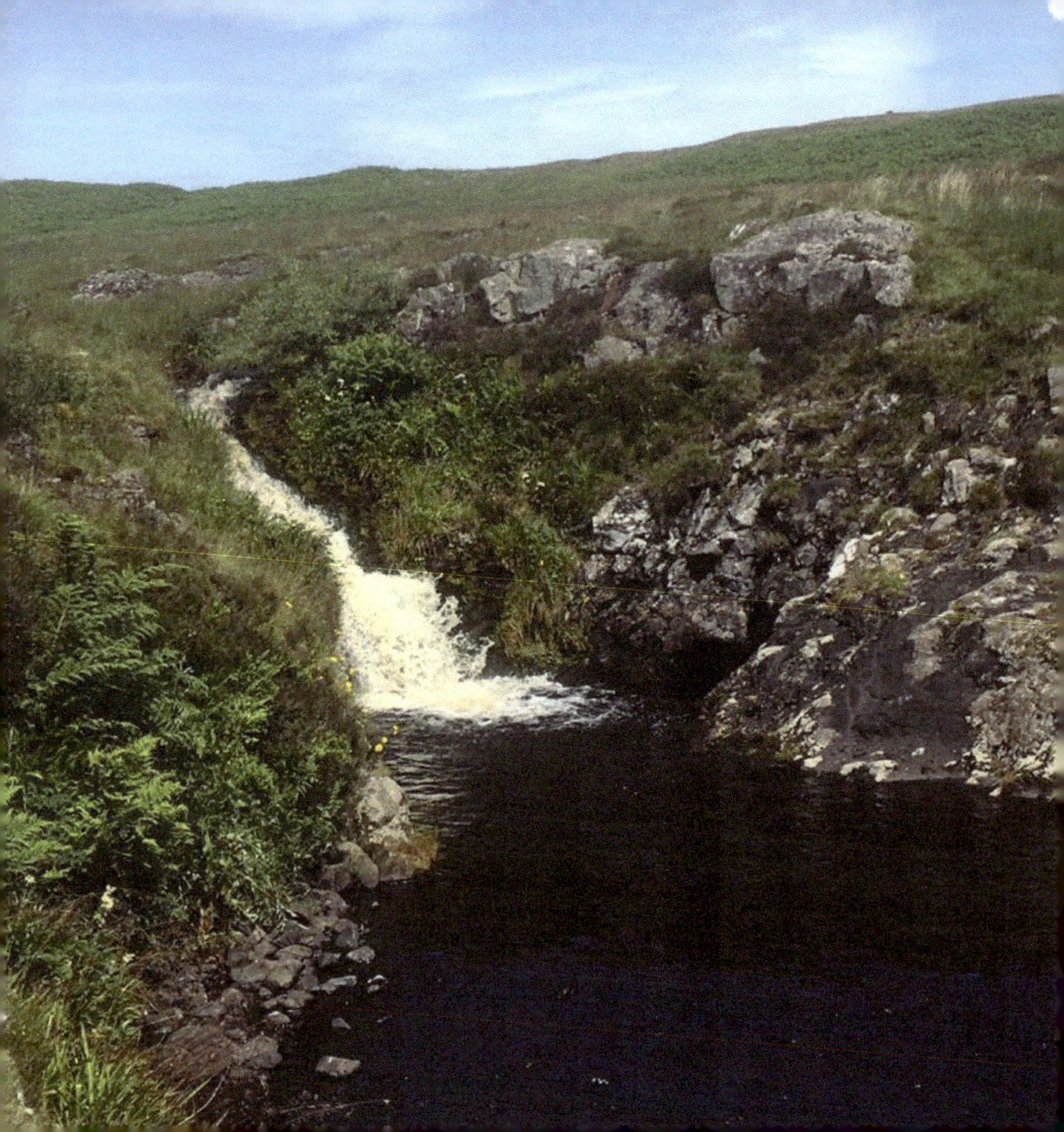

Lost And Forgotten Frontiers and a Camel!

I wrote earlier about how, from c.700 AD to c.1124 and the coronation of David I, Stirling lay on the former frontier between Pictland and its successor Alba, and Northumbria. A much less well-known frontier lies 10 miles to the south on the Earl's Burn. The earldom in question was The Lennox, one of the oldest in Scotland and with very shadowy origins. It seems likely to have been carved out from British Kingdom Alt Clut following the Viking capture of Dumbarton Rock after a three month siege in 870. The core of the kingdom relocated to Govan, renamed itself Strathclyde, and extended as far south as modern Cumbria.

The early history of the Lennox is unknown, and we have only one vague reference to it as an independent state from the 11th century. A King of Munster called Muirchertach mac Tairdelbaig meic Taidc meic Briain appears to have taken tribute from The Lennox, which is described as one of three distinct polities (Alba and Strathclyde being the other two). He also received a camel from the Scottish King Edgar (David I's elder brother)! That's it—no King of The Lennox, and then, when the area reappears, it's an Earldom under the Scottish King. This period of Scottish history is full of small shadowy kingdoms that flicker in and out, all driven by strong men who in turn are beaten by other strong men (chaos, in other words). Did people fight and raid over this frontier? We don't know, but on occasion I now swim here and never give much thought to either frontiers or camels!

Keep going south to the Carron Valley for an abandoned court.

NS 71390 87315

The Gowk's Stanes
An Abandoned Court

Beyond the frontier of The Lennox and Alba lies an odd geological feature: the Gowk's Stanes, meaning either the fool's or the cuckoo's stones in Scots. These lie close to the wonderful Loup o' Fintry; an amazing waterfall (and a not bad dook) with a 94 feet drop. The stones look like a small row of stumpy standing stones, but are entirely natural. The stones lie close to the parish boundary between St Ninians and Fintry, and also to Gallows Knowe. It seems likely this is the remains of an open-air local court where the rulers of Fintry Castle exercised their power—where justice was seen and heard to be done with the guilty punished at the knowe. As the notorious Braxfield said, 'Yir a clever chiel, but nane the waur o' a guid hingin'.

As one might imagine, such courts were very common across Scotland, but they begin to fizzle out in the 16th centuries. They tend to be called 'couthal' or 'tulach', from the Gaelic. Couthal names became 'cowden' in Scots, and these are quite rare around Stirling (there is only one, and it's at Buchlyvie at Cowden Knowes (NS 58029 94340), a modest, lumpy hill range). By contrast, tulachs became either Tull- or Touch, and these are all over Stirling and Clackmannanshire (e.g. Touch Estate, Tullibody and Tillicoultry). Presumably our Gowk's Stanes court had a similar name which is now lost to time. As to why these open-air courts were abandoned, have you been to Scotland? It's cold and wet, so of course the powerful wanted to keep warm and dry while passing sentence.

Keep going down the hill round to Fintry for either a lovely meal in the Fintry Inn or a glorious homemade ice cream in the Courtyard Café!

NS 66144 86357

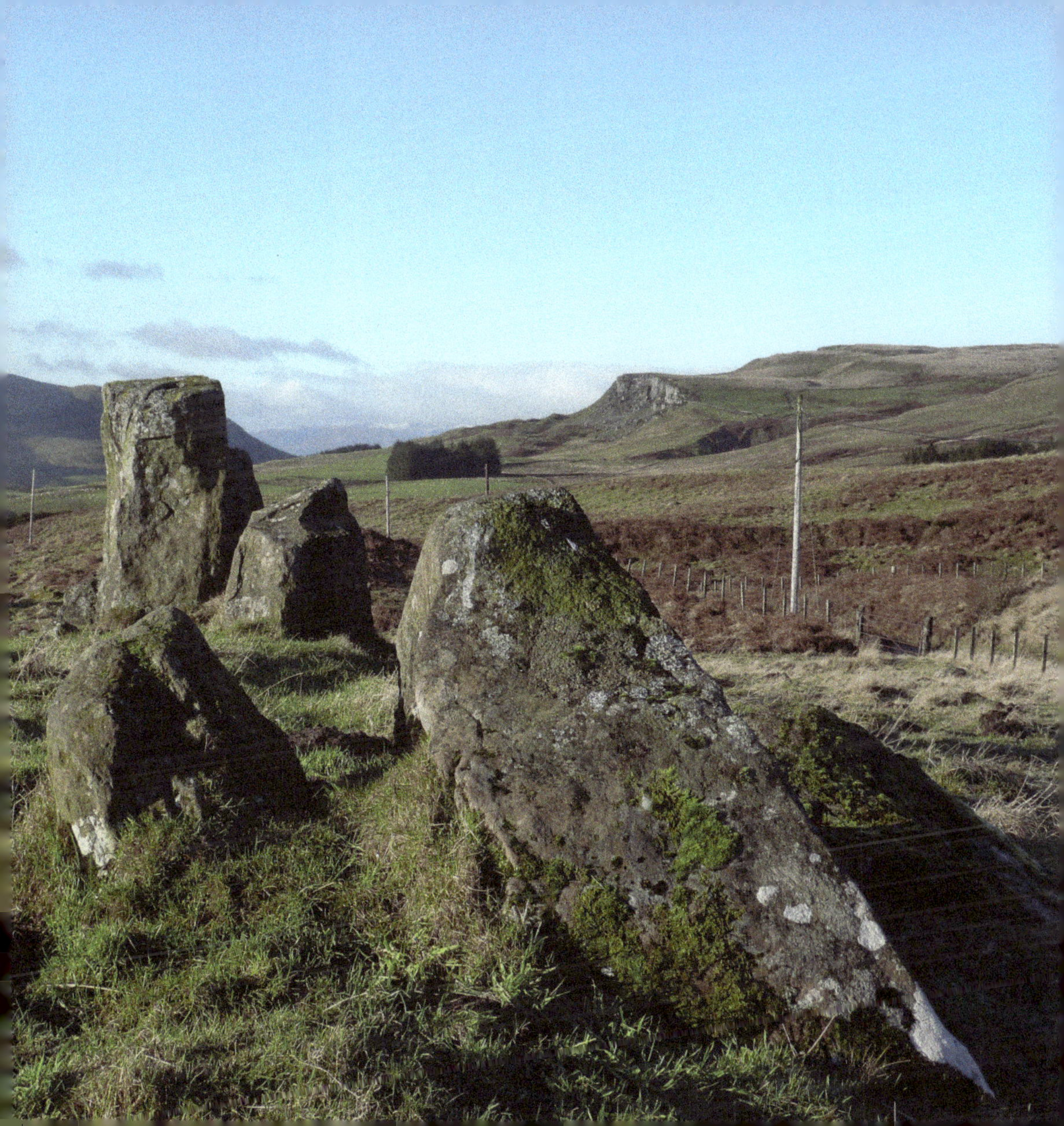

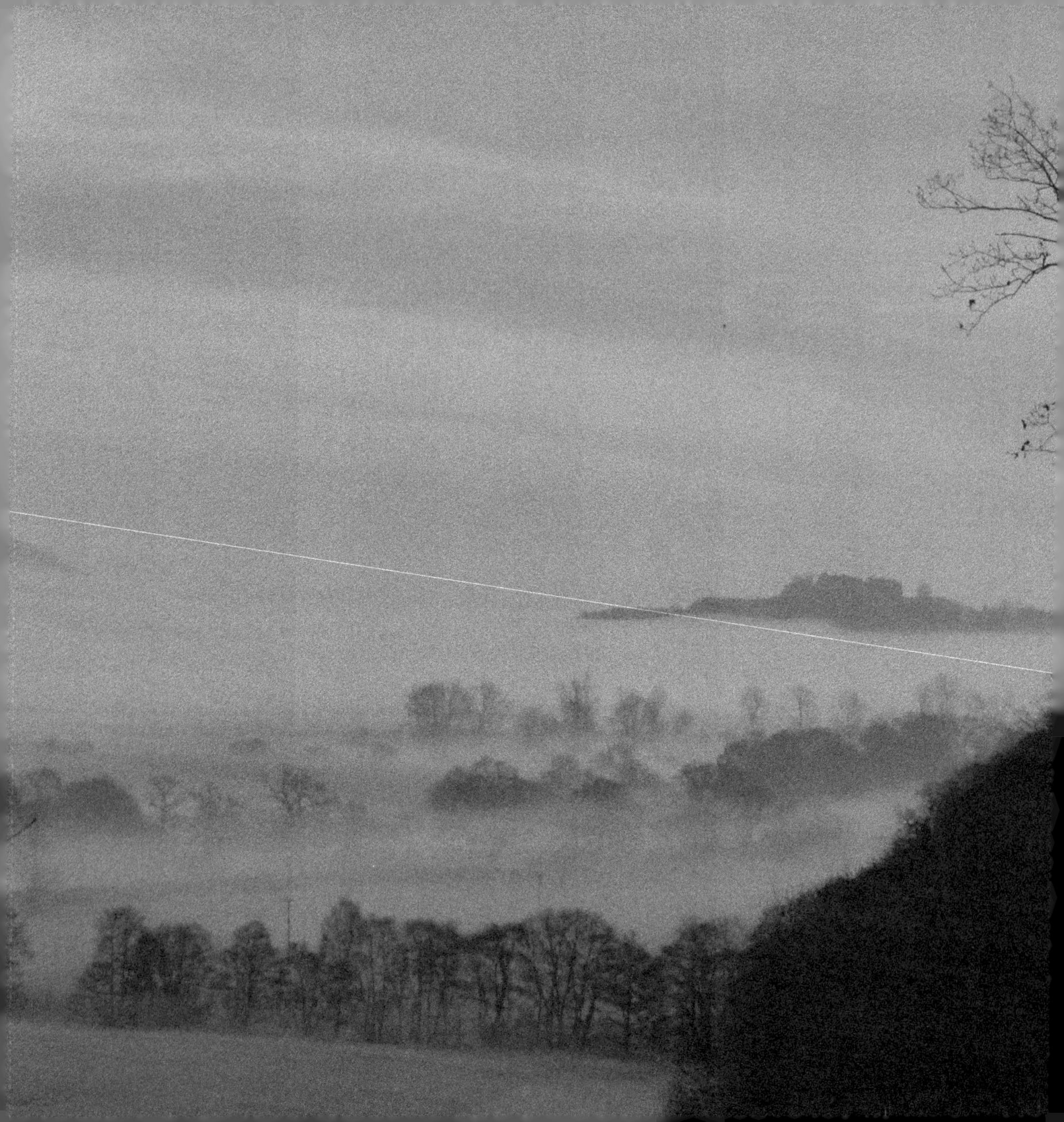

Another Lost Cemetery
Baston Burn

This is best done in winter because of the tick-ridden bracken that is, in places, eight feet high. You've been warned! It illustrates one of the key issues about archaeology; we don't know what we're looking at till we dig it. Opinion has varied on Baston Burn for decades: for some it was a burial cairn, for others a substantial roundhouse. The owner is the former Forestry Commission, and they also wanted to know what they had—so enter stage left your local archaeological hero with the expenses covered. We dug here over a few years to work out what was going on, and the first surprise was it had been flattened to build a medieval farm.

But what was it? The clue, of course, is in the title—a cemetery, so a cairn. Normally cairns are built to be seen from a distance, to celebrate the dead. This one is on a ridge overlooked by another hill; it's not on the highest point, and is very easily missed. So what's going on? It was built around 3,000–4,000 years ago by farmers using the Touch Hills for summer grazing. The winter was out as the location is too exposed. This is known as transhumance (your new word for the day). Cattle would be driven up the ridge to graze the fresh spring pasture and the cairn marked the route; it celebrated ancestors who had carved a life from this landscape and who were commemorated each year as the community went up and then back. It has an incredible view, but what makes the spot even more special is that under the cairn was something even older—8,000 year old charcoal from amongst the very first people in Scotland. This spot and its view has been enjoyed since the glaciers melted. Will you love it too?

N3 73924 93693

An Illegal Church and a Minister on the Run!

The Scottish Reformation always astonishes me. We heard about the wanton destruction in the name of iconoclasm at the Church of the Holy Rude, and the persecution of 'witches' and the banning of Christmas. The same dogged mindset led to the fight for religious freedom (though this really meant the right of mostly men to be exactly the type of Protestant they wanted to be). In the late 17th century, Charles II—and later his brother, James VII—wanted to control worship. Scots Protestants rallied behind the National Covenant, which guaranteed their freedom (indeed, both Charles I and II signed it), and people who defended these rights were known as Covenanters. Events eventually took a more violent turn, and there were armed rebellions—around 100 Church of Scotland ministers were executed for treason (The Killing Times). And so people were forced to worship in secret locations, and these were called Conventicles.

James Ure led Conventicles across the moor to the south of Kippen (where he had been Minister), and one location was this fabby little gorge beneath a prominent rock called Dugald's Tower. Ure even took 200 armed volunteers to the Battle of Bothwell Brig in 1679. Following their defeat, Ure went on the run in the hills above Kippen and a reward of £100 was offered for his capture, but no one betrayed him. His mother was arrested and died in Glasgow Tolbooth, while his wife and young child were held for questioning for four weeks in the Edinburgh Tolbooth. All of this was forgiven after William of Orange came to power and former religious extremists (or freedom fighters) became members of society again, and the Kippen Conventicles became Victorian tourist spots.

NS 65342 93317

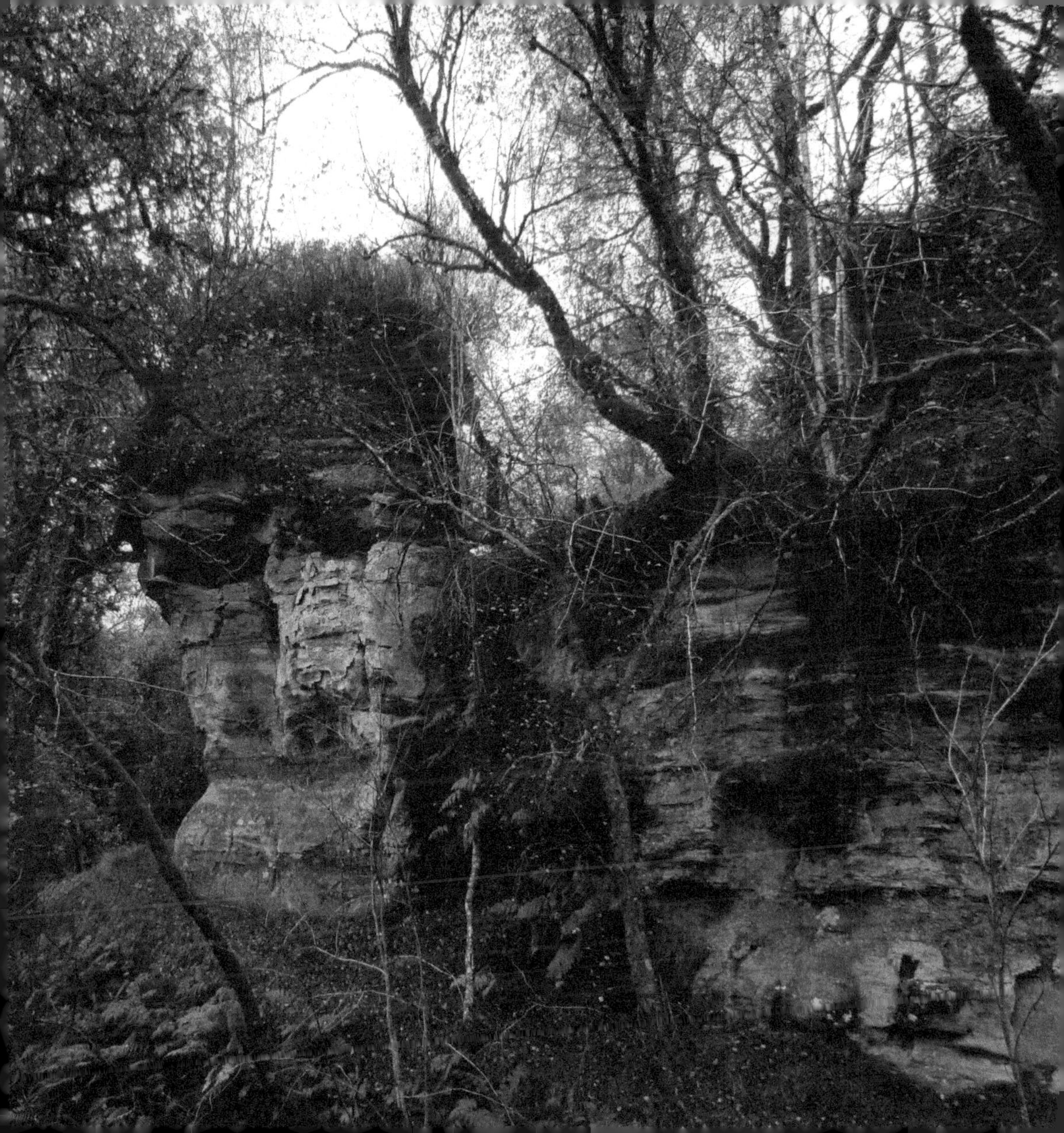

Acknowledgements

The following people kindly provided images for the book:

- Fiona McLean provided the introductory image of the Marches
- Raymond Dormer provided Image 7
- Roy Sexton provided Image 26
- Tom Astbury provided Image 27

Massive thanks to Therese McCormick who waded through my terrible prose and produced the maps.

Endnotes

1. And oddly, the first time it's ever been celebrated... as we forgot the date (it was sometime between 1124-1127) and I argued we could tie to David I's coronation, and so an anniversary was born!

2. The 'Holy Rude' is an archaic name for the Holy Cross.

3. We don't know much about Mary, her age, or what she died of—simply that she was old.

4. As I write this, the clock was just knocked down by an elderly driver, and its future is uncertain.

5. Famously, Scotland prosecuted a larger percentage of our population than anywhere else in Europe.

Image Credits

All images are from the author's private collection unless otherwise stated.

Frontispiece: Stirling, showing Stirling Castle and the National Wallace Monument. Photo by Neostalgic at Unsplash, and reproduced under the Unsplash Licence.

Introduction: The author (left) on the 2024 Walking of The Marches as a Birlawman and Warden of the Eastern Marches, with former Provost Mike Robbins (centre) and Fraser Sinclair carrying Stirling's official mace. Image is Copyright © Fiona McLean and reproduced by kind permission of the copyright holder.

Dedication: Stirling Castle overlooking Stirling. Photo by Almudena at Pixabay, and reproduced under the Pixabay Licence.

Page vi: Map of Stirling City produced by Therese McCormick, and reproduced by her kind permission.

Page viii: Map of Stirling and its Environs produced by Therese McCormick, and reproduced by her kind permission.

Page x: The Ballengeich Sally Port.

Page 3: Empty niches on the church of the Holy Rude.

Page 4: The foundation of the Watch House.

Page 7: Bastion under excavation. Image is Copyright © Raymond Dormer, and appears by kind permission of the copyright holder.

Page 8: The Edmonstone family Plantation, from Thomas Staunton St. Clair, *A Residence in the West Indies and America* (London, 1834). Image is in the Public Domain.

Page 11: The grave of Dr Graham Gordon.

Page 12: Raymond Dormer's grandfather on the eagles in the 1930s.

Page 15: The Forbes family plot.

Page 16: The Broad Street tea pavilion, prior to dismantling.

Page 19: The Tolbooth's secret bell.

Page 20: The Hangman's House, from William Drysdale, *Auld Biggins of Stirling, its Closes, Wynds, and Neebour Villages* (Stirling, 1904). Image is in the Public Domain.

Page 23: Cowane's bee boles.

Page 24: David I on Stirling High School.

Page 27: The Viking glaring at the wolf.

Page 28: The Guildry 4.

Page 31: A replica of Wallace's sword.

Page 32: The Alhambra Theatre roof.

Page 35: The golden lion.

Page 36: The Thieves' Pot.

Page 39: The site of the Dominican Priory.

Page 40: The Provost Pool sculpture.

Page 43: The Spittal Hill section of the Causeway.

Page 44: A 6,000 year old oyster.

Page 47: The Allan Water island.

Page 48: The hermitage staircase.

Page 51: Prize winning *Ledum palustre*, courtesy of Roy Sexton. Image is Copyright © Roy Sexton, and appears by kind permission of the copyright holder.

Page 52: The Abbey Ford by Tom Astbury. Image is Copyright © Tom Astbury, and appears by kind permission of the copyright holder.

Page 55: The Argyll and Sutherland Highlanders War Memorial.

Page 56: The Road Round Coxet Hill.

Page 59: Kings Park cemetery under excavation.

Page 60: The hogback from James Sturk Fleming's *Old Nooks of Stirling* (Stirling, 1898). Image is in the Public Domain.

Page 63: Bruce's Well from James Sturk Fleming's *Old Nooks of Stirling* (Stirling, 1898). Image is in the Public Domain.

Page 64: The threshold to Hayford House.

Page 67: The wall and the lade.

Page 68: The King's Deer Dyke.

Page 71: The Falleninch field towards Stirling Castle.

Page 72: The Randophfield standing stone.

Page 75: An 18th century graffiti tag.

Page 76: The Player Factory clock.

Page 79: The oak pegs from Bannockburn House's 17th century roof.

Page 80: Dunblane's Royal Horseshoe.

Page 83: Gartincaber House from William Drysdale, *Auld Biggins of Stirling, its Closes, Wynds, and Neebour Villages* (Stirling, 1904). Image is in the Public Domain.

Page 84: The entrance to the Blair Drummond Estate.

Page 87: An extract from James Stobie's 1783 map of Scotland, provided by the National Map Library of Scotland. Reproduced with the permission of the National Library of Scotland.

Page 88: The Easter Polmaise ice house.

Page 91: The Dunmore wind pump.

Page 92: The Earl's Burn.

Page 95: The Gowk's Stanes.

Page 96: The view from Baston Burn ring cairn.

Page 99: Dugald's Tower.

Page 107: Author photo from personal collection of Dr Murray Cook.

About the Author

Dr Murray Cook is Stirling Council's Archaeologist. He lives in the city with a long-suffering wife, three teenage girls and two pesky but loveable cats. He has undertaken numerous excavations across the region and published over 50 books and articles. He won a Stirling's Provost Award in 2018 for his work for the Council, where he has helped raise over £300,000 to be spent on community archaeology and research, and was even invited to see the Queen at Holyrood Palace, along with a few hundred others! He has appeared on several TV programmes, and has sometime even been paid. He writes a regular column in the *Stirling Observer*, is an Honorary Research Fellow at Stirling University, a Fellow of the Society of Antiquaries of Scotland, runs an occasional course at Forth Valley College on Stirling and likes to do it in ditches (archaeology that is!). He also co-runs regular training digs open to all under the name *Rampart Scotland*. In March 2025 he was presented with the Outstanding Contribution to the City Award at the Stirling Business Awards 2025. If you share Murray's passion for the past, why not look up his weekly blog *Stirling's Archaeology*? It's free to join.

For details of new and forthcoming books from Extremis Publishing, including our monthly podcasts, please visit our official website at:

www.extremispublishing.com

or follow us on social media at:

www.facebook.com/extremispublishing

www.linkedin.com/company/extremis-publishing-ltd-/

www.ingramcontent.com/pod-product-compliance
Ingram Content Group UK Ltd.
Pitfield, Milton Keynes, MK11 3LW, UK
UKHW050902170425
457514UK00003B/5

9 781739 484590